What does it mean to

Attention Deficit Hyperactivity Disorder

Louise Spilsbury

www.heinemann.co.uk/library
Visit our website to find out more information about Heinemann Library books.

To order:
📞 Phone 44 (0) 1865 888066
📠 Send a fax to 44 (0) 1865 314091
💻 Visit the Heinemann Bookshop at www.heinemann.co.uk/library to browse our catalogue and order online.

First published in Great Britain by Heinemann Library,
Halley Court, Jordan Hill, Oxford OX2 8EJ,
a division of Reed Educational and Professional Publishing Ltd.
Heinemann is a registered trademark of Reed Educational and Professional Publishing Ltd.

OXFORD MELBOURNE AUCKLAND
JOHANNESBURG BLANTYRE GABORONE
IBADAN PORTSMOUTH (NH) USA CHICAGO

© Reed Educational and Professional Publishing Ltd 2001
The moral right of the proprietor has been asserted.

All rights reserved. No part of this publication may be reproduced, stored in a retrieval system, or transmitted in any form or by any means, electronic, mechanical, photocopying, recording, or otherwise, without either the prior written permission of the publishers or a licence permitting restricted copying in the United Kingdom issued by the Copyright Licensing Agency Ltd,
90 Tottenham Court Road, London W1P 0LP.

Designed by AMR
Illustrated by David Woodroffe
Originated by Dot Gradations
Printed by Wing King Tong in Hong Kong.

ISBN 0 431 13922 9
05 04 03 02 01
10 9 8 7 6 5 4 3 2 1

British Library Cataloguing in Publication Data
Spilsbury, Louise
    What does it mean to have Attention Deficit Hyperactivity Disorder (ADHD)?
    1. Attention-deficit hyperactivity disorder
    I.Title II.ADHD (attention deficit hyperactivity disorder)
    616.8'589

Acknowledgements
The publishers would like to thank the following for permission to reproduce photographs: Corbis/Philip Gould, p.15; Corbis Stock Market, p.25; Zoe Dominic, p.23; Powerstock Zefa/Fotostock, Int, p.18, /Sharpshooters, p.5; Science Photo Library/Gaillard, Jerrican, p.4, /Garry Watson, p.7; Stone/Peter Cade, p.16; Telegraph Colour Library/Genna Naccache, p.19.

The following pictures were taken on commission for Heinemann: Trevor Clifford, pp.8, 9, 10–14, 17, 20–22, 24, 28, 29; John Walmsley, pp.26, 27.

The pictures on the following pages were posed by models who do not have ADHD: 4, 5, 9–27.

Special thanks to: Elspeth, Andrew, Steven, Adam, Yolanda and Joe.

The publishers would also like to thank Dr Marian Perkins, Consultant Child Adolescent Neuropsychiatrist, and Julie Johnson, PHSE Consultant Trainer and Writer, for their help in the preparation of this book.

Cover photograph reproduced with permission of Science Photo Library/ Galliard Jerrican.

Every effort has been made to contact copyright holders of any material reproduced in this book. Any omissions will be rectified in subsequent printings if notice is given to the publishers.

Contents

What is attention deficit hyperactivity disorder?	4
What causes ADHD?	6
Identifying ADHD	8
What is ADHD like?	10
Meet Lucy and Sam	12
Coping with ADHD	14
Help yourself!	16
Medicines	18
Meet Jessie and Roz	20
Living with ADHD	22
At school	24
At home	26
Meet Joe	28
Glossary	30
Helpful books and addresses	31
Index	32

Any words appearing in the text in bold, **like this**, are explained in the Glossary.

What is attention deficit hyperactivity disorder?

Attention deficit hyperactivity disorder (ADHD) is a **condition** that causes a person to have difficulties learning, behaving and getting on with others. Young people with ADHD have three main difficulties – **inattention**, **hyperactivity** and **impulsiveness**. These words are tricky.

- Inattention: people who are inattentive find it hard to concentrate on one thing at a time. They have trouble paying attention to anything for very long.
- Hyperactivity: people who are hyperactive cannot sit still. They always seem to be moving around.
- Impulsiveness: people who are impulsive don't think before they say or do things. They say and do things without really thinking about what might happen afterwards or how other people might feel.

Attention deficit disorder

You may have, or you may know someone who has attention deficit disorder (ADD). People who have ADD have some of the same difficulties as people with ADHD. They have trouble learning and concentrating and they may be impulsive. The difference is that they don't have difficulties with hyperactivity.

At school we all have to learn to sit still, pay attention, get on with our work and wait our turn. Until they know they have ADHD and begin to get the help they need, children with ADHD find all of these things very difficult.

Some people find that having ADHD can be a positive thing – you might be able to use some of that boundless energy to help you score the winning goal for your school team!

Getting on with it

All of us do or say things without thinking sometimes, or we find it hard to concentrate or keep still when we should be getting on with our work. The difference for children with ADHD is that things like this happen often and can happen wherever they are – at home, at school or out on a trip.

Facts about ADHD
- Experts believe that around one or two children out of every hundred have ADHD.
- Anyone can have ADHD, but more boys than girls seem to have it.

What causes ADHD?

Lots of people think that ADHD is a new condition. In fact, the reason we hear more about it today is that doctors have become better at recognizing the symptoms and understanding the causes. They think that people have ADHD because of tiny, subtle differences in the way that parts of their **brain** work. In many people with ADHD it seems that the parts of the brain that deal with, say, paying attention, have not developed in the usual way.

How does the brain work?

Your brain controls the rest of your body. It controls how you think, learn and feel. Messages from your brain travel to different parts of your body to tell them what to do in different situations. Inside your brain, different areas deal with different kinds of messages. Some areas respond to signals from your **sense organs** (eyes, ears and so on) so you can see, hear, touch, speak and move. Other parts of the brain are involved in dealing with your thoughts, feelings or memories.

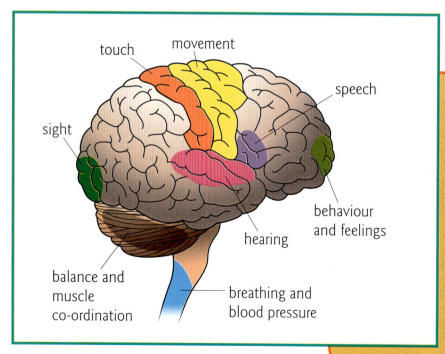

*Your brain is the most complicated **organ** in your body. Each area of the brain is responsible for different jobs in the body.*

Scientists are discovering new information all the time about how the brain works. In the future they may be able to explain exactly what causes ADHD and find new ways of helping people who have it.

Chemicals and the brain

The brain is made up of billions of tiny **nerve cells**. They connect to each other to sort out information that comes into the brain, work out thoughts and make decisions. For example, when you touch something hot, nerve cells send a message to the brain telling you to take your hand away.

Nerve cells rely on **chemicals** to be able to do their different jobs. The chemicals are made in different parts of the brain in tiny but exact amounts. They affect the way that messages are sent between the nerve cells. There are nerve cells in the parts of the brain that control a person's **impulsiveness**, concentration and awareness of time. Some people who have ADHD have too much or too little of a chemical in these parts. This affects how these parts of the brain control their behaviour. People with ADHD sometimes behave differently from most other people because of tiny chemical differences like these in particular parts of their brain.

Identifying ADHD

Sometimes, parents spot the signs of ADHD when their child is still a toddler, before they go to school. They may wonder why the child cannot sit still long enough to finish a game, or runs around out of control at home and at playgroups or other people's houses. Teachers are often the first to notice that something is wrong. They see lots of children every day and they can tell when someone is behaving or learning differently from other children of the same age.

When a parent is concerned, their first step is usually to take the child to see their local doctor. If the doctor suspects that the child may have ADHD, she or he will send the child to see a **specialist**. These are special doctors who have had a lot of training and experience with difficulties like ADHD. They can tell if a person really has ADHD.

Some mothers of young children who have ADHD describe them as small whirlwinds, dashing around breaking toys and disrupting everything in their paths!

The whole picture

There is no simple way of finding out if someone has ADHD. The first thing a specialist usually does is rule out other possible reasons for the child's behaviour. For example, they may check that the child can see and hear properly. If a child cannot see or hear very well, this may be the reason they are not paying attention at school – not because of ADHD.

When other possible causes have been ruled out, the specialist gathers all the information they can about the child. They talk to the young person to find out how they feel. They also find out how the child behaves at school and at home. The specialist may also talk to the child's family, their family doctor, and to teachers. They gradually build up a picture of the child to help them to decide whether they have ADHD.

Specialists gather information about a person who may have ADHD by talking to them, their family and sometimes their teacher.

What is ADHD like?

What does it really mean to be **inattentive**, **hyperactive** or **impulsive**? Here we look at some of the ways these affect children's lives. All children are different and all children with ADHD have different kinds and levels of difficulties. Some children may only have a few difficulties. People with **severe** symptoms may find it very hard to control their ADHD. Many children grow out of their symptoms, or learn how to control them.

Inattention

Most children with ADHD try very hard to concentrate, but find that their mind moves on to other subjects. For example, some find it hard to do their homework. They may forget to copy down what the homework is, or to bring home the books they need to do it. When they settle down to get on with it, they find that however hard they try, they cannot concentrate. Even though they may be quite capable of doing their work, they fail to finish it, or hand it in full of mistakes.

Some people say having ADHD is a bit like looking at the world through a kaleidoscope. There are lots of different thoughts, pictures and sounds going round in their head, making it impossible to concentrate on one thing only.

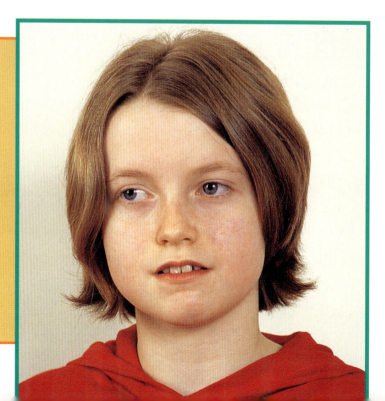

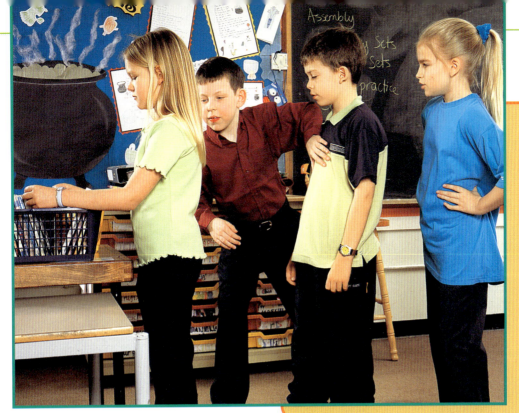

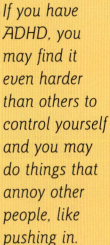

If you have ADHD, you may find it even harder than others to control yourself and you may do things that annoy other people, like pushing in.

Hyperactivity

People who are hyperactive seem to be full of energy. They just cannot sit still. They may dash about, talking non-stop. At school they may be on the move all the time – tapping their feet, getting up and down to go to the cloakroom or to sharpen a pencil. They may try to do several things at once, moving on to a new piece of work or project before they have finished the last one.

Impulsiveness

People who are impulsive may hurt people's feelings because they say things about others without thinking first. They may do dangerous or annoying things because they do not think before they act. They may put themselves in danger, by climbing high trees or running across a busy main road. Sometimes they may annoy other people because they find it hard to wait their turn in the dinner queue or in games lessons. They may push in or hit out when they are upset because they find it hard to control how they feel and act.

Meet Lucy and Sam

My name is Lucy and my son Sam is ten years old. He has attention deficit hyperactivity disorder. We didn't find out he had ADHD until he was nine. Up until then he had not had any real difficulties at school. Then suddenly he began to have problems with his schoolwork and he was getting into trouble. His father and I were often called in to see the Head about him.

We thought Sam might have some kind of problem with learning, like **dyslexia**, so we took him to a **specialist** for a check-up. She spent a lot of time with Sam, talking to him and doing tests to see what he knew and understood. She asked his school and us to answer lots of questions about Sam. Sam's dad was away at that time so I saw her alone. I was really upset when she first told me that Sam had ADHD. I was worried that Sam was going to have a really hard time ahead of him. My husband and I took Sam to see a second specialist. She told us that Sam did have ADHD, but that it was not **severe**.

The specialist said Sam should take an ADHD medicine called **Ritalin**. This didn't really help much and he was still getting into trouble. He had some sessions with a **counsellor** to help him understand what ADHD is. This also gave him a chance to talk over how he felt about it all. Sam also saw a special schoolteacher every day for a year, and she helped him find ways of learning that suited him. Then we decided he should move schools. He moved from a small primary school to a large, busy secondary school where children play a lot of sport.

He loved the new school straight away. He seemed to grow out of the ADHD. He no longer needed the medicine or the extra teaching help. He has gone from having real trouble with his writing to doing very well in English. He now plays in the school rugby team and really enjoys it. He still talks all the time – he's a real chatterbox and great fun to be around. He loves music, and comedy programmes on TV. He also loves animals and hopes to work with them when he grows up.

Coping with ADHD

All children with ADHD are different – just as all children are different. Each child needs different kinds and amounts of help. It is a bit like going for a pair of glasses. You don't just get glasses that are meant for anyone who is short-sighted. Eyes are tested and glasses are made to suit the individual.

Emotions can be hard to cope with. Think about how you feel when you are angry or upset about something. It helps all of us to have someone to talk problems over with.

Most children who have ADHD are helped in a variety of ways. Some have help learning to control their behaviour, or advice on how to get on with other people. They may have help with schoolwork, to learn ways of concentrating on their work or completing it. Some children may also take medicine to help them to calm down and concentrate. Sometimes people with ADHD feel that no one understands them. They may feel frustrated that they cannot concentrate. It may help if they can talk to someone about how they feel, and who can help them understand about their **condition**.

Help is at hand

Some children who are told they have ADHD may feel as if they have been given a bad label. They may feel different from their classmates, or feel that there is something wrong with them. Most, however, are relieved to know why they have been feeling upset or frustrated. They are glad to know they can get help to improve things.

The fact that someone has ADHD does not change who they are. Taking medicine and having help from a new teacher are no different from wearing braces on your teeth or glasses for your eyes. The treatment they have is just a tool to help them focus and pay attention. Just as braces make your teeth straight or glasses help you see, the medicine and support given to children with ADHD are just a way of helping them get on with their lives.

If you have ADHD, you may find that it gets better as you find ways to control it. Most people with ADHD learn to deal with the difficulties they have, and to make the most of the things they are good at.

Help yourself!

People with attention deficit hyperactivity disorder are often the best people to think of ways of solving their problems. With encouragement, most people can come up with ideas or plans to help themselves.

Many start off with a bit of detective work. They keep a diary of their week, noting down any difficult times they had. Many children with ADHD understand what went wrong after something has happened. The difficult bit for them is stopping it from happening again. With a diary, they can look back to see what caused the problem and think of ways of changing things. They may do this alone or with the help of a parent or teacher. For example, a person may get into trouble at school because they keep leaving their desk. They might decide to try using up some of their energy in other ways. They may do more sport during the day, move around only at set times, or teach themselves to fidget in their seat rather than leaving it.

Exercise is good for all of us, but it can be especially useful if you have ADHD. Doing sport or just running around at break-time can help you settle in class afterwards.

Having a little extra time to do a test can give young people with ADHD a much fairer chance to show what they have learned.

Ways of learning

We all learn in different ways. For example, some people remember things better if they are written down; others are happier to have things explained to them. People with ADHD often find learning hard. They are just as clever as other people – it is just that they learn things in a slightly different way. They may feel happier if they can break a project into several small pieces of work. It is easier to concentrate on shorter pieces and it is encouraging to finish work successfully. Some need longer to finish work than other people. For them, being given longer to complete a test can make the difference between passing and failing.

Lots of children with ADHD also find it helps if they can use a computer. They find that computer programs present information in ways they find interesting, which helps to hold their attention. Some people with ADHD have trouble presenting work neatly. This is not a problem if they can type it up on a computer.

17

Medicines

Think about how you feel when you are really tired and you have not had enough sleep. Maybe you get a bit fidgety, cannot concentrate properly on schoolwork, feel worn out and perhaps a bit snappy. Then you have a good night's rest, and these feelings go away. For some children with ADHD, this is what it feels like when they take medicine to help their **symptoms**. They find they are able to concentrate and pay attention in class.

Not all children with ADHD take medicine, but some people find that it really helps. There are a number of different medicines for ADHD. Children may take different kinds of medicines in different amounts. The most common one is called **Ritalin**. Children usually take a small number of Ritalin tablets every day. Even if medicines are **prescribed**, they should never be the only form of help offered.

If you have ADHD, your doctor will check on you regularly to see if you still need medicine. Some children grow out of ADHD and stop taking medicine. Other children find that the medicine helps them learn ways of coping with ADHD so that eventually they need less, or even none at all.

Natural remedies

Many people like to take what we call 'natural remedies' – medicines made from plants or other natural sources. Some people find that taking tablets with **vitamins** or **herbs** can help their ADHD. It is often hard to prove whether these natural remedies help, but many people believe they do.

Doing without

Some parents and children do not like the idea of taking medicines for ADHD. They say that children react differently to medicines and that medicines can have **side-effects**, such as making some children lose their appetite or keeping them awake at night. Some children find that medicines don't help anyway, or that they feel worse when they take them. Some doctors say that side-effects can be handled by reducing the amount of the medicine taken. Even so, some people still prefer to work on their ADHD without the help of medicines. It is important that people choose the kind of help that suits them best.

Some children find that taking medicines for ADHD helps them at home and at school. They feel happier and more hopeful because they know they can do some things right.

19

Meet Jessie and Roz

I'm Jessie. I'm nine years old. When people ask me about ADHD I remember that I used to hate school. When I was seven years old my mum says I wasn't really naughty but I sang and talked all the time and I stopped everyone else from doing their work. I remember that I didn't like the work. I couldn't do the writing and I never finished in time so I had to stay in at break-times to finish it. I didn't care about that because I didn't have many friends then. Some of the other girls in my class said I was silly and bossy and they wouldn't let me play with them.

I don't really understand what ADHD is, but I was glad when the doctor told us that I had it. I was happy that there were other people like me and that the doctor said he could help me. I went to a special small class for a while. The teacher was very nice and never shouted at me. She helped me do my work in bits so I could do it more easily. She let me use the computer a lot as well, and I like using the computer.

My name is Roz and I'm Jessie's big sister. Jessie can be great but she can also be a nuisance. I get fed up with her when she barges in on me when I'm in my bedroom with my friends. Once I got really cross with her. My mum got me to write down all the good things I could think of about her. I wrote down things like 'Jessie is very friendly when she meets someone new' and 'She is very gentle with our cat.' She was really pleased. Now she tries hard to remember to knock on my door. I have put a notice on the door reminding her to knock and ask to come in first.

Jessie and I do a lot together. We both like listening to music and she likes to bounce around in the sitting room dancing. She also likes cooking but it's hard for her to read what the cookbooks say. So I write recipes out for her in simple, clear steps so she can cook cakes and other things pretty much by herself.

Living with ADHD

It can be tough living with ADHD. Some children feel that parents are always getting at them, teachers pick on them and other children don't like them. This can lead to them having very low **self-esteem**. That means they do not like themselves very much. They may feel angry with themselves for behaving as they do. They may cover up or even hide their feelings by pretending not to care. They may become angry and hit out because they are frustrated.

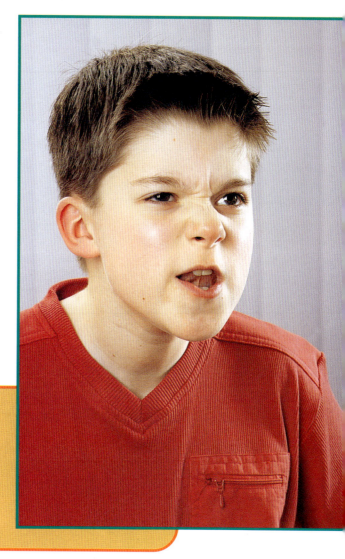

Some people criticize children who have ADHD and their families because they think the child is rough, or badly behaved. The real problem is that they don't understand what ADHD is.

Life can also be difficult for the people who live, play or work with children who have ADHD – their parents, brothers and sisters, teachers or classmates. Brothers and sisters may get fed up because the child with ADHD seems to get all the attention. Classmates may be cross because the child with ADHD spoils their games. It helps to remember that children with ADHD do not choose to act as they do. It's just that sometimes they can control themselves and sometimes they cannot. With the help of others, like parents, friends and teachers, they can learn to control themselves more.

22

How does it feel?

Although it can get them down at times, some young people with ADHD feel that it gives them special advantages over other people. Many say they are more outgoing and ready for action than lots of other people they know. They are often curious and very determined. The effects of their ADHD may get them into trouble sometimes, but they can also be useful. For example, some people think children with ADHD are bossy because they like taking charge of other people. They may find this annoying, but others may be happy to go along with them. They are glad to know someone who is good at coming up with ideas for games and taking the lead.

Most children with ADHD don't let it stop them doing what they want to do. If they join a drama club, they may not be able to remember enough words to perform in a play, but they may be very good at designing or making costumes or scenery.

At school

We all know how hard it is to get on with our work if something is distracting us. Young people with ADHD find it even harder to concentrate. At school they might not be able to focus on what the teacher is saying if, for example, traffic is going past outside, someone is turning pages of a book nearby, or a clock is ticking loudly.

Tactics that work!

Here are some of the tactics children with ADHD say can help them concentrate at school.
- Sit away from distractions; for example, sit away from windows or doors, or near the teacher.
- Ask teachers to repeat tasks or write them down.
- Keep desks clear of anything but the books you are working on.
- Break tasks down into smaller parts, so you can concentrate on one thing at a time.
- Agree with an adult or friend on a special signal they can use to remind you to get back to work when they see you daydreaming.

Some children find that it helps if their teacher uses a secret signal to remind them to pay attention. This teacher touches the boy's desk as she passes. No one notices, but it reminds him to get on with his work!

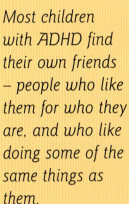

Most children with ADHD find their own friends – people who like them for who they are, and who like doing some of the same things as them.

Making friends

Lots of children with ADHD make friends easily, just like other people. Friends can be a big help. They may get annoyed by some of the things a person with ADHD does, but they don't reject them. After all, we all do things that bother our friends sometimes. The best thing to do is explain to people the things they do which you don't like, but say that you still like them as a friend. That way they understand that it is just the behaviour you dislike, not them.

Sometimes children with ADHD get bullied, or even become bullies themselves out of anger or frustration. If you do see someone being picked on or bullied, for whatever reason, you should tell a teacher. If you are worried about getting into trouble with the bullies, tell the teacher when no one else is around. People who are being bullied need a friend and you are doing the right thing if you help someone who is being made unhappy.

At home

If you have ADHD, life can feel a bit chaotic and out of control at times. It can help if life at home has some kind of routine and order. That may mean getting up, having meals or going to bed at the same time every day.

This family has a breakfast-time race to see who can finish first. This helps the youngest child, who has ADHD, eat up in time so that he, his brother and sister are not late for school!

This is not always as simple as it sounds. Some young people with ADHD find it hard to do things at set times. In the morning they may get up slowly and make everyone else late, or disrupt breakfast by getting up and down from the table. It is not fair to them to let them get away with such behaviour just because they have ADHD. Most children just need help to learn to do things differently. Some find that the promise of a treat, such as fifteen minutes of television, is enough to help them concentrate and get on with their meal.

Hassle-free homework

Lots of young people with ADHD find that it helps to do their homework at the same time every day and in the same, quiet place. They may ask their families to help them stop any distractions, perhaps by taking phone calls for them or by turning the television off.

Many also keep a checklist by their table or desk to help them focus on their work. For example, some people who are **impulsive** make mistakes because they leap in and answer questions without thinking them through. Their checklist could remind them to take their time and to jot down any ideas they have for an answer before writing it up. It might also include a reminder for them to ask an adult to rephrase a question if they are finding it hard to understand. You might like to try some of these things yourself!

If you have a book to read for school, it is easier to concentrate if you find somewhere you can be on your own, away from distractions. Make sure you are comfortable as well!

Meet Joe

I'm Joe and I am fourteen years old now. I found out I had ADHD when I was about nine. I was getting into a bit of trouble at school. I went to see a **specialist** who asked me lots of questions and I filled out a kind of form. She told us I had ADHD.

When people ask me about ADHD I tell them that it's not something which is necessarily bad. It's a disorder where you can sometimes be disruptive, and you can lose track of what you should be doing, and you can sometimes be noisy. Sometimes you lose control over what you're doing and you behave in a way other people wouldn't.

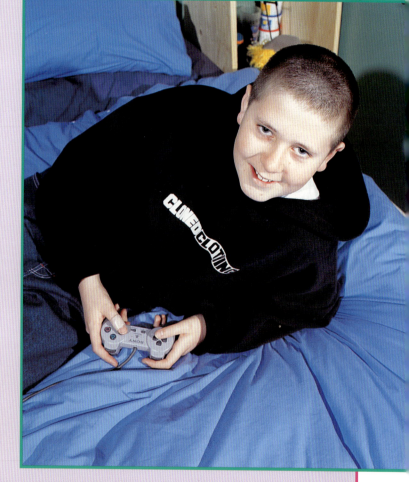

Sometimes I lose concentration at school. I can't always get on with my work and then I joke about. When I get told off I get wound up. My school knows all about my ADHD so if I'm getting stressed out they just say go out and cool down for a bit. They don't see it as a bad thing – they just make allowances for me sometimes.

The only downside about ADHD is remembering to take my **Ritalin** tablets. They are a kind of medicine to help me concentrate and slow down a bit – I have to admit I do tend to rush around from first thing in the morning till last thing at night. I have to take the tablets in the morning, and then at lunchtime, so if I am at school I have to keep some in the medical room. I also have to take tablets at teatime and bedtime, so I have to remember to take them with me if I go to a friend's house to stay.

Otherwise ADHD is a good thing because it makes me more energetic and lively. I've got lots of energy. I don't like things where there isn't much going on. I like being with my friends – I get bored watching TV or being on my own. I like to be doing things. I like most sports, but especially football and ice hockey. One of the things I like most is playing the drums. It's a good way of letting off steam. I'd like to be a drummer in a band when I grow up.

Glossary

brain organ inside your skull. It is the centre of your nervous system and it controls the rest of your body. It tells the rest of your body what to do and deals with thoughts, ideas, feelings and memories.

chemicals great variety of substances which can do many different things. Some chemicals in the brain help to transmit messages from one nerve cell to another.

condition word used to describe an illness or disease that a person has for a long time, perhaps all their life. It is also often used to describe an illness that a person is born with.

counsellor person who is trained to help people with their problems by talking to them and offering advice

dyslexia people who have dyslexia have certain difficulties with reading, writing or spelling. They may also have trouble reading numbers or notes on a sheet of music.

herbs plants that can be used in cooking or in medicines

hyperactivity/hyperactive people who are hyperactive cannot stay still. They always seem to be moving around. Their minds may be overactive as well.

impulsiveness/impulsive people who are impulsive do not think before they say or do things. They say or do things without thinking about what might then happen or how other people might feel about it.

inattention/inattentive people who are inattentive find it hard to keep their mind on one thing. They have trouble paying attention to anything for very long.

nerve cells tiny bundles that pass information between the different parts of the brain

organ part of the body that has an important job. Your organs include your brain, heart, lungs and liver.

prescribe when a doctor tells someone to take a medicine

Ritalin name of one of the kinds of medicine that may be given to people who have ADHD. Such medicines do not cure people but may help to ease the symptoms. Medicines should be used along with other forms of support to help people learn new ways of behaving.

self-esteem when someone feels good about themselves, they have high or good self-esteem

sense organ organ that gives us our sense of touch (skin), sight (eyes), hearing (ears), smell (nose) or taste (mouth and tongue)

severe very serious. Someone who has severe ADHD may find it very hard to cope with life at an ordinary school because they need a lot more help controlling their behaviour.

side-effects unwanted effects of taking a medicine. A medicine usually gives good effects, such as lessening the symptoms of a disease. It may also give unwanted 'side-effects', such as headaches, stomach-aches or sleeplessness.

specialist someone who has a lot of training and experience in a particular subject. Specialists in ADHD know all about ADHD and understand its complicated symptoms.

symptom something that your body feels or experiences that tells someone that you may have a disease or illness. Symptoms of ADHD include inattention, hyperactivity and impulsiveness.

vitamin nutrient that helps to keep our bodies healthy

Helpful books and addresses

BOOKS
Think about Having a Learning Disability, Margaret and Peter Flynn, Belitha Press, 1998

I Am Me And You Are You, Althea Braithwaite, A & C Black, 1999

When It's Hard To Learn, Judith Condon, Franklin Watts, 1998

ORGANIZATIONS AND WEBSITES
Attention Deficit Disorder/Hyperactive Disorder Family Support Group UK
c/o 1A High Street
Dilton Marsh
Westbury
Wiltshire BA13 4Dl
Telephone: 01373 826045

ADDISS (ADD Information Services)
PO Box 340
Edgeware
Middlesex HA8 9HL
Telephone: 020 8906 9068
Fax: 020 8959 0727

LADDER (National Learning and Attention Deficit Disorders Association)
PO Box 700
Wolverhampton
WV3 7YY

The above groups offer support, information and advice to people in the UK with ADHD and ADD.

IN AUSTRALIA
ADDult Association (NSW) Inc
PO Box 472
Sutherland NSW 2232
Telephone: 02 9540 3300

Australian Department of Health and Aged Care
Central Office
GPO Box 9848
Canberra ACT 2601
Telephone: 02 6289 1555
Freecall: 1800 020 103
Fax: 02 6281 6946
e-mail: webmaster@health.gov.au

Index

ADD (attention deficit disorder) 4
ADHD (attention deficit hyperactivity disorder) 4–29
anger and frustration 11, 14, 15, 22, 25

behaviour, unacceptable 11, 22, 26, 28
bossy behaviour 20, 23
brain 6–7
bullying 25

calming down 14, 28
causes of ADHD 6–7
chemicals in the brain 7
computers 17, 20
concentration 4, 5, 7, 10, 14, 18, 24, 27, 28
coping with ADHD 14–15, 22–3
counsellors 13

diary keeping 16
doctors and specialists 6, 8, 9, 12–13, 20, 28
dyslexia 12

emotions 14
energy 5, 8, 11, 16, 29

family life 21, 22, 26
fidgeting 11, 16, 18
friendships 25
hearing and vision problems 9
homework 10, 27

hyperactivity 4, 10, 11

impulsiveness 4, 7, 10, 11, 27
inattention 4, 10

learning difficulties 4, 17

medicines 13, 14, 15, 18–19, 29

natural remedies 19
nerve cells 7

people affected by ADHD 5
positive side of ADHD 5, 23, 29

Ritalin 13, 18, 29

schools and schoolwork 4, 12, 13, 14, 17, 18, 20, 22, 24–5, 28
self-esteem, low 22
self-help 16–17
sense organs 6
side-effects of medicines 19
sport 5, 13, 16, 29
support from others 14, 15
symptoms of ADHD 8–9, 10

talking over problems 13, 14
time, awareness of 7, 28

vitamins 19

writing skills 13

Titles in the *What does it mean to have/be* series include:

Hardback   0 431 13924 5

Hardback   0 431 13921 0

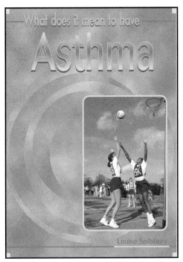

Hardback   0 431 13920 2

Hardback   0 431 13922 9

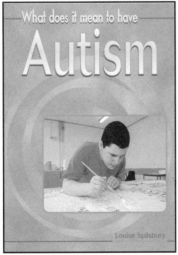

Hardback   0 431 13925 3

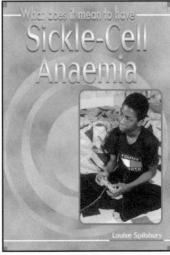

Hardback   0 431 13923 7

Find out about the other titles in this series on our website www.heinemann.co.uk/library

THE GREAT TR

Walker's Haute Route
Chamonix to Zermatt

by
Andrew McCluggage

About the Author

Andrew McCluggage is an outdoor writer and photographer. After 20 years as a corporate lawyer, he decided to do something interesting and started writing walking guidebooks.

His first book was Walking in the Briançonnais, covering a beautiful part of the French Alps. Since then, he has written a variety of books including walking guides for the Tour du Mont Blanc and the Tour of the Écrins National Park (GR54).

Andrew is from Northern Ireland but spends a lot of time each year in the Briançonnais.

Publisher: Knife Edge Outdoor Limited (NI648568)
12 Torrent Business Centre, Donaghmore, County Tyrone, BT70 3BF, UK
www.knifeedgeoutdoor.com

©Andrew McCluggage 2019
All photographs: ©Andrew McCluggage 2019
First edition 2019

ISBN: 978-1-912933-02-0

A catalogue record for this book is available from the British Library

All rights reserved. No part of this publication may be reproduced in any form without the prior written consent of the publisher and copyright owner.

Maps 1a, 1b, 1c, 1d, 2b and 2c: extracts reproduced from IGN 1:25,000 maps with the permission of IGN (Authorisation no. 60.18019). ©IGN-2018. All other maps: extracts reproduced from 1:50,000 maps with the permission of SwissTopo (BA19021). Reproduction is not permitted (Reproduction interdit).

The names GR®, PR® and GRP® are registered trademarks. ©FFRP for all GR®, PR® and GRP® paths. In France, FFRandonnée and its tireless team of volunteers maintain the waymarking on many walking paths. Their familiar red/white marks make navigation easier. More information on the network of paths marked by FFRandonnée can be found at www. monGR.fr.

All routes described in this guide have been recently walked by the author and both the author and publisher have made all reasonable efforts to ensure that all information is as accurate as possible. However, while a printed book remains constant for the life of an edition, things in the countryside often change. Trails are subject to forces outside our control: for example, landslides, tree-falls or other matters can result in damage to paths or route changes; waymarks and signposts may fade or be destroyed by wind, snow or the passage of time; or trails may not be maintained by the relevant authorities. If you notice any discrepancies between the contents of this guide and the facts on the ground, then please let us know. Our contact details can be found at the back of this book.

Front cover: A hiker savours the view from the Europaweg (Stage 13b)
Introduction page: Lac de Moiry (Stage 9a)

Contents

Getting Help	1
Introduction	3
Direction and Start/Finish Points	4
Guided or Self-Guided	5
When to go	6
Using this Book	8
Itinerary Planner	10
14 Days: Option 1	11
14 Days: Option 2	12
13 Days	13
12 Days	13
11 Days	14
10 Days	14
Variant Stages	15
Accommodation	16
Camping	18
Accommodation Listings	20
Food	28
Facilities	29
Getting There	32
On the Route	34
Costs	34
Weather	34
Maps	34
Paths and Waymarking	35
Water	36
Escape Routes	36
Pastous	36
What to take	37
Safety	40
General Information	42
Wildlife	44
Flowers	46
Route Summary	47
Route Description	53
1a Chamonix to Argentière	55
1b Argentière to le Tour	57
1c Le Tour to Col de Balme	59
1d Col de Balme to Le Peuty	61
v1d Col de Balme to Refuge les Grands	63
v1e Refuge les Grands to Col de la Forclaz	65
2a Le Peuty to Col de la Forclaz	67

2b Col de la Forclaz to Arpette	71
v2b Col de la Forclaz to Champex (via Bovine)	75
2c Arpette to Champex	77
3 Champex to le Châble	79
4 Le Châble to Cabane du Mont Fort	81
5 Cabane du Mont Fort to Cabane de Prafleuri	85
v5 Cabane du Mont Fort to Cabane de Prafleuri (via Col de la Chaux)	89
6a Cabane de Prafleuri to Refuge de la Gentiane	91
6b Refuge de la Gentiane to Arolla	93
v6b Refuge de la Gentiane to Arolla (via Cabane des Dix)	97
7a Arolla to la Gouille	99
7b La Gouille to les Haudères	101
7c Les Haudères to la Sage	103
8 La Sage to Cabane de Moiry	105
v8 La Sage to Barrage de Moiry (via Col de Torrent)	109
9a Cabane de Moiry to Barrage de Moiry Junction	111
9b Barrage de Moiry Junction to Zinal	113
10 Zinal to Gruben	115
v10a Zinal to Hôtel Weisshorn	119
v10b Hôtel Weisshorn to Gruben (via Cabane Bella-Tola)	121
11 Gruben to St-Niklaus	125
12 St-Niklaus to the Europahütte	129
v12a St-Niklaus to Grächen	133
v12b Grächen to the Europahütte	135
v12c St-Niklaus to Randa (via Herbriggen)	137
v12d Randa to the Europahütte	139
13a The Europahütte to Täschalp	141
13b Täschalp to Zermatt	145
v13 Randa to Zermatt (via Täsch)	147
Zermatt Day Walks	149

WARNING

Hills and mountains can be dangerous places and walking is a potentially dangerous activity. Many of the routes described in this guide cross exposed and potentially hazardous terrain. You walk entirely at your own risk. It is solely your responsibility to ensure that you and all members of your group have adequate experience, fitness and equipment. Neither the author nor the publisher accepts any responsibility or liability whatsoever for death, injury, loss, damage or inconvenience resulting from use of this book, participation in the activity of mountain walking or otherwise.

Getting Help

Emergency Services Numbers: France 112; Switzerland 144.

Distress Signal

In the Alps, the signal that you are in distress is 6 blasts on a whistle spaced over a minute, followed by a minute's silence. Then repeat. The response that your signal has been received is 3 blasts of a whistle over a minute followed by a minute's silence. At night, flashes of a torch can also be used in the same sequences. **Always carry a torch and whistle.**

Signalling to a Helicopter from the Ground

Help Required
Raise both arms in the shape of a 'Y'

Help Not Required
Raise one arm and extend the other arm down and outwards.

A mountain rescue helicopter lands at a refuge high up in the French Alps

The many glaciers are a key characteristic of the WHR

Introduction

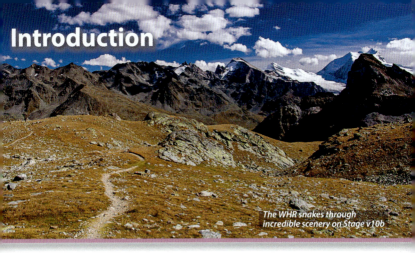

The WHR snakes through incredible scenery on Stage v10b

If the Tour du Mont Blanc (TMB) is the most famous trek in the Alps, the Walker's Haute Route (WHR) is surely a close runner-up. Comparison between the two treks is regularly made as they are often considered to be sisters: many who have completed, and loved, the TMB look to the WHR for their next trekking challenge. The WHR is slightly tougher than the TMB so it is the logical next step. To be spoken about in the same breath as the exquisite TMB is in itself a huge compliment, however, many claim (with some justification) that the WHR is superior both in terms of scenery and experience.

Whilst the TMB is a circular route, the WHR is linear: an uninterrupted journey between the two most famous mountaineering locations in the Alps and the two most famous mountains in the Alps. Travelling from Chamonix in France to Zermatt in Switzerland, you will start at Mont Blanc and finish at the Matterhorn. Fair weather views of either of these peaks would certainly rank as highlights of anybody's walking career, but the WHR also exhibits a dizzying array of other jagged Alpine peaks. In fact, you pass the largest collection of snowy 4000m summits in the Alps: Mont Blanc, Grand Combin, the Weisshorn, the Zinalrothorn, the Dom, the Täschhorn, the Breithorn and the Matterhorn, to name a few.

Distance	206km
Altitude Gain/Loss	14,055m/13,487m
Mountain Passes	12
Days	10 to 14
Highest Point	Col de Prafleuri (2987m)

Almost daily, you cross incredible mountain passes (or cols) enabling passage from magnificent valley to magnificent valley. And there are exquisite alpine pastures, sparkling azure lakes, and carpets of wild flowers, the like of which you will never have seen before.

But there are perhaps two other key characteristics of the WHR. Firstly, the wildness: the WHR has sections which are fabulously remote and rugged. It is an intense and adventurous mountain experience. Secondly, the magnificent glaciers: they are everywhere you look on almost every stage. Furthermore, you get extremely close to some of them. And as the trek lasts between 10 and 14 days, you can savour them.

You will live and breathe these scenic delights, night and day, because you need never leave the mountains: fabulous accommodation is available in beautiful alpine villages and remote mountain huts, spaced out along the route. Places with views that most people dream of but few will ever see. Places that you will never forget. Places that will leave you with remarkable memories. If this trek is not on your bucket list then you are, as we say in Ireland, 'barking mad'.

Although the WHR is a popular trek, it rarely feels as busy as the TMB. This huge swathe of the Alps is easily large enough to swallow the many walkers that descend upon it each summer. Get a reasonably early start and you will find yourself largely alone for much of the day. You will occasionally pass, or be passed by, other trekkers but these meetings can be as fleeting as you wish. And at the end of the day, on arrival at your resting place, often high above the valleys, you will likely meet some of the people you came across earlier. Then bonds are formed over dinner or a drink. Like the TMB, the WHR has a fine reputation as a sociable trek.

> **Ask the Author**
>
> If you have any questions which are not answered by this book, then you can ask the author on our Facebook Group, 'Haute Route Q&A'

Notwithstanding statistics published elsewhere, we find the main WHR route to be 206km in length with 14,000 metres of ascent and 13,500 metres of descent. 12 magnificent mountain passes are crossed. These figures are consistent with statistics obtained online from Switzerland Mobility. In addition, there are 13 incredible variants described here, totalling 137km. The variants are summarised in a separate table in the Itinerary Planner.

If all that sounds intimidating, then do not worry: with the right preparation, planning and approach, the WHR is manageable for most people of reasonable fitness. Yes it is a challenge but it is a realistic one. And that is where this guide comes in: most of what you need to know to prepare for the WHR is here within these pages. And the entire route is described in detail to guide you on the trek itself. Furthermore, unlike other books, this one contains Real Maps: for each stage, there is a 1:25,000 or 1:50,000 scale map, licensed from the relevant mapping agencies.

Direction and Start/Finish Points

Traditionally, the WHR is walked west to east, and the vast majority travel that way, so this book describes it in that direction. Although it could also be tackled in the other direction, there are some good reasons why few people do this. Firstly, by walking east you walk towards the rising sun which falls first on east facing slopes: this means that you benefit from morning shade for most of the steep climbs (which are often west facing). The Alps get hot in the summer so this makes a big difference to your strength and stamina. Secondly, the Matterhorn is arguably the highlight of the whole trek so it is wonderful to save the best for last. Furthermore, Zermatt is probably a nicer place than Chamonix in which to spend a few days at the end of the trek.

Nevertheless, some people do undertake the WHR east to west and that approach is not without merit: some prefer not to meet the same people every day and walking against the flow solves this problem. The Real Maps in this book, with numbered waypoints, make the route descriptions simple to follow in reverse.

It is also possible to walk shorter sections of the WHR. There are many access points along the route which have public transport including Champex, Sembrancher, le Châble, Arolla, les Haudères, Zinal, and St-Niklaus. You could start at any of these places and walk a few sections. Or you could skip sections by leaving the route at one of these access points and using public transport to resume at another point.

Guided or Self-Guided

The question we get asked the most is whether to walk independently or with a guided group. The answer is a personal one, depending upon your own particular circumstances and requirements. For many, the decision to organise the trek themselves, and to walk independently, can be almost life changing, opening the door for more difficult challenges in the future. There is much satisfaction to be gained in planning and navigating a trek yourself and the sense of achievement on completion is to be savoured.

In theory, most could walk independently: although it is slightly harder than the TMB, the WHR is within the capabilities of most reasonably fit people and the trail is mostly waymarked so, in normal conditions, route-finding is largely straightforward (with a few exceptions). However, the self-guided trekker usually carries his own pack and is responsible for all decisions which need to be made daily such as pacing; which way to go at junctions; when to stock up with food and water; and choice of route in bad weather. For some, this will be too great a burden on top of the physical effort required simply to walk. For those walkers, a guided group is a great solution: the tour company typically organises food, accommodation and transfer of luggage each night. And the guide makes all the decisions, enabling the walker to concentrate on the walking. There are a number of tour companies operating guided trips on the WHR but not all offer the full route.

The incredible Lac de Louvie (Stage 5)

When to go

Normally the WHR can be tackled from late June to late September. For the more adventurous, it can sometimes be undertaken in October.

Late June can be the most beautiful time for walking. The weather is sunny and warm and the peaks are frequently at their most photogenic, still fully frosted with snow. Summer haze has not yet arrived so visibility is generally excellent with wide-ranging views. And there are carpets of spring wildflowers. Of course, there is occasionally rain at this time of year but this usually lessens as the season progresses. And there are fewer visitors so accommodation is easier to find and significantly, the mountains are more peaceful. That said, as overall visitor numbers increase and reservations in July/August become harder to secure, the amount of early season walkers seems to increase each year.

As with all Alpine treks, in some years, high cols can be snow-covered until early July, making parts of the WHR difficult and/or dangerous: in such conditions, crampons and/or an ice axe might be helpful. There are now some very light, compact crampons available which weigh a mere 300g so carrying them just in case is not the burden it once was. Microspikes are another lightweight option for early-season trekkers.

July and August is the main summer season when the high cols are normally passable on foot. It can be hot, sometimes reaching more than 30°C. Mornings often start with clear and sunny skies and heat up as the sun gains height. If there is to be cloud or haze, often this will arrive in the afternoon when thunderstorms are more likely. Start walking early in the morning to complete the main climb while the temperature is cooler. This is the busiest season on the WHR and it is advisable to make bookings well in advance as accommodation is often full, particularly at weekends. Do not turn up without a reservation and expect to find accommodation. Furthermore, in this period, it can be difficult to alter your plans once on the trek: a change to one day's schedule has a chain reaction across the rest of your trip and refuges/gîtes may not be able to accommodate the changes.

Month	Pros	Cons
Late June	Pleasant temperatures; Frequent sunny skies; Good visibility; Wild flower season; Fewer visitors	High cols and peaks occasionally inaccessible due to snow
July/August	Generally reliably fine weather; High cols normally passable; Basking in the sun!	The hottest period; Sometimes hazy; Visitor numbers highest; Afternoon thunderstorms
September	Pleasant temperatures; Frequent sunny skies; Excellent visibility; Fewer visitors; Autumn colours	Accommodation closes as the month progresses; Shorter days; Cooler evenings; Occasional snowfall
October	Autumn colours; Frequent sunny skies; Excellent visibility; Fewer visitors	Greater possibility of snow; Much accommodation closed; Short days; Cold mornings and evenings

September is the new June! It can be the best month for walking as the weather is often more settled than in summer. Skies are usually clear and visibility excellent. Daytime temperatures are still warm but evenings get cooler and the days get shorter. The odd flurry of snow is possible, particularly later in the month, but they tend to clear quickly. From the start of September, visitor numbers reduce so the mountains are quieter and there is less demand for accommodation. However, from mid-September some accommodation starts to close for the season so check availability in advance.

October is a very beautiful time, with autumn colours on full display in the warm low light. Careful planning is needed to undertake the route at this time of year. As the month progresses, the possibility of snowfall on the cols increases which could make them impassable or dangerous. Check the weather forecasts carefully along the way. If fresh snow is forecast, do not set out. Much accommodation would be closed so you could carry camping gear. You would need to be prepared to carry more food as there would be fewer places to stock up. October is for experienced trekkers only.

Even in summer snow is possible at altitude (Stage 5)

The beautiful statue of an Ibex at Sorebois (Stage 9b)

Using this Book

This book is designed to be used by walkers of differing abilities. Many guidebooks for long-distance treks rigidly divide the route into a fixed number of long day stages and it is for the walker to break down those stages to design daily routes which suit his/her abilities. This book, however, has been laid out differently to give the trekker flexibility: it divides the route into 23 shorter sub-stages which can be combined to design daily routes to meet your own specific needs.

Each of the 23 sub-stages covers the distance between one accommodation option and the subsequent one. Almost every accommodation option on the entire route is the start/finish point of a sub-stage. You can choose how many of these sub-stages you wish to walk each day. Each sub-stage has its own walk description, route map, elevation profile and beautiful photos.

The labelling of the sub-stages uses a combination of numbers and letters. It is a simple system but requires a little bit of explanation. Firstly, every sub-stage has a number between 1 and 13: each number represents one day of our standard 13 day schedule. As the standard 13 day schedule is broken down into sub-stages, these sub-stages are also given letters (e.g. "6a"). Take a look at the detailed Itinerary Planner below and all should become clear.

The Itinerary Planner includes a range of tables outlining Suggested Itineraries of 10, 11, 12, 13 or 14 days. In each table, the maths have been done for you so there is no need for you to waste time (and mental strength!) working out daily distances, timings and height gain.

Of course, the Suggested Itineraries are only suggestions. You can shorten or lengthen your day in any number of ways to suit yourself: just decide how many sub-stages you want to walk that day. It is up you. As there is accommodation at the end of each sub-stage, it easy to design your own bespoke itinerary and adjust it on the ground as you go along.

For example, day 6 of the standard 13 day route involves walking sub-stages 6a and 6b. But you could decide to extend day 6 by walking sub-stages 6a, 6b and 7a all on the same day. Or you might be tired and decide to shorten your day by walking only sub-stage 6a. With other guidebooks, you would have to work out how to split stages yourself, involving some complicated maths to plan distances and times going forward. This guide, however, does all the hard mental work for you.

In this book:

Timings indicate the approximate time required by a reasonably fit walker to complete a stage. They do not include stoppage time. Do not get frustrated if your own times do not match these: everyone walks at different speeds. As you progress through the trek, you will soon learn how your own times compare with those given here and you will adjust your plans accordingly.

Distance is measured in kilometres (km) to match maps and signposts in Europe. One mile equates to 1.6km.

Place names in brackets in the route descriptions indicate the direction to be followed on signposts. For example, "('Champex')" would mean that you follow a sign for Champex.

Ascent or descent numbers are the aggregate of all the altitude gain or loss (measured in metres) on the uphill or downhill sections of a sub-stage. As a rule of thumb, a fit walker climbs 300 to 400m in an hour.

Elevation profiles tell you where the climbs and descents fall on the route. The profile lines have been deliberately drawn in varying thickness purely for aesthetic purposes. Read the elevations off the top of the lines.

The following abbreviations are used:

MB	Mont Blanc
WHR	Walker's Haute Route
TMB	Tour du Mont Blanc
TL	Turn left
TR	Turn right
SH	Straight ahead
N, S, E and W, etc.	North, South, East and West, etc.

The view from the Augstbordpass (Stage 11)

Itinerary Planner

Stages

Grand Combin and Mont Blanc seen from Col de Louvie (Stage 5)

Stage	Start	Time (hr)	Km	Ascent (m)	Descent (m)	Max. Altitude (m)
1a	Chamonix	2.50	9.3	274	67	1252
1b	Argentière	1.25	4.0	252	43	1475
1c	Le Tour	2.00	4.3	738	0	2191
1d	Refuge du Col de Balme	1.75	5.2	0	865	2191
2a	Le Peuty	0.75	2.1	200	0	1526
2b	Col de la Forclaz	6.00	12.2	1149	1048	2665
2c	Arpette	0.75	2.4	0	161	1627
3	Champex	4.00	14.1	192	837	1470
4	Le Châble	6.25	12.3	1665	30	2456
5	Cabane du Mont Fort	6.50	13.9	960	754	2987
6a	Cabane de Prafleuri	1.50	3.2	194	399	2803
6b	Refuge de la Gentiane, la Barmaz	5.50	13.0	641	1090	2918
7a	Arolla	2.00	4.8	252	426	2141
7b	La Gouille	1.25	4.0	20	404	1834
7c	Les Haudères	0.75	2.3	230	13	1667
8	La Sage	5.75	10.9	1676	518	2867
9a	Cabane de Moiry	2.25	6.8	96	548	2825
9b	Barrage de Moiry Junction	3.50	8.9	478	1177	2836
10	Zinal	6.25	16.8	1270	1126	2874
11	Gruben	7.25	17.1	1096	1787	2892
12	St-Niklaus	7.75	17.2	1862	725	2696
13a	Europahütte	3.50	8.9	512	619	2264
13b	Täschalp	3.75	12.3	298	850	2347
Finish	Zermatt					

Suggested Itineraries

The unforgettable sight of the Matterhorn (Stage 13a)

14 Days: Option 1

Our most leisurely approach for those with time. The first two days are easier to allow your body to adjust to the demands of the trek. Day 3 is the first challenging stage but it is followed by another easier one.

Day	Stages	Time (hr)	Km	Ascent (m)	Descent (m)
1	1a, 1b	3.75	13.3	526	110
2	1c, 1d, 2a	4.50	11.6	938	865
3	2b	6.00	12.2	1149	1048
4	2c, 3	4.75	16.5	192	998
5	4	6.25	12.3	1665	30
6	5	6.50	13.9	960	754
7	6a, 6b	7.00	16.2	835	1489
8	7a, 7b, 7c	4.00	11.1	502	843
9	8	5.75	10.9	1676	518
10	9a, 9b	5.75	15.7	574	1725
11	10	6.25	16.8	1270	1126
12	11	7.25	17.1	1096	1787
13	12	7.75	17.2	1862	725
14	13a, 13b	7.25	21.2	810	1469

14 Days: Option 2

This option is useful for those arriving in Chamonix later in the day as you can warm up with a half-day walk of 9km and overnight in Argentière. Days 2 and 3 are progressively more difficult but then the easy Day 4 allows recovery before the harder stages to come.

Day	Stages	Time (hr)	Km	Ascent (m)	Descent (m)
1	1a	2.50	9.3	274	67
2	1b, 1c, 1d, 2a	5.75	15.6	1190	908
3	2b, 2c	6.75	14.6	1149	1209
4	3	4.00	14.1	192	837
5	4	6.25	12.3	1665	30
6	5	6.50	13.9	960	754
7	6a, 6b	7.00	16.2	835	1489
8	7a, 7b, 7c	4.00	11.1	502	843
9	8	5.75	10.9	1676	518
10	9a, 9b	5.75	15.7	574	1725
11	10	6.25	16.8	1270	1126
12	11	7.25	17.1	1096	1787
13	12	7.75	17.2	1862	725
14	13a, 13b	7.25	21.2	810	1469

Taking in the view (Stage 11)

13 Days

Our standard schedule which successfully divides the trek up into manageable stages. It is a tried and tested approach which is perfect for many walkers.

Day	Stages	Time (hr)	Km	Ascent (m)	Descent (m)
1	1a, 1b, 1c, 1d	7.50	22.8	1264	975
2	2a, 2b, 2c	7.50	16.7	1349	1209
3	3	4.00	14.1	192	837
4	4	6.25	12.3	1665	30
5	5	6.50	13.9	960	754
6	6a, 6b	7.00	16.2	835	1489
7	7a, 7b, 7c	4.00	11.1	502	843
8	8	5.75	10.9	1676	518
9	9a, 9b	5.75	15.7	574	1725
10	10	6.25	16.8	1270	1126
11	11	7.25	17.1	1096	1787
12	12	7.75	17.2	1862	725
13	13a, 13b	7.25	21.2	810	1469

12 Days

This ramps things up a little. Days 5 and 6 are hard ones but your legs should be well walked in by then. The itinerary also offers an overnight stay at the wonderfully serene Refuge de la Gentiane.

Day	Stages	Time (hr)	Km	Ascent (m)	Descent (m)
1	1a, 1b, 1c, 1d	7.50	22.8	1264	975
2	2a, 2b	6.75	14.3	1349	1048
3	2c, 3	4.75	16.5	192	998
4	4	6.25	12.3	1665	30
5	5, 6a	8.00	17.1	1154	1153
6	6b, 7a, 7b, 7c	9.50	24.1	1143	1933
7	8	5.75	10.9	1676	518
8	9a, 9b	5.75	15.7	574	1725
9	10	6.25	16.8	1270	1126
10	11	7.25	17.1	1096	1787
11	12	7.75	17.2	1862	725
12	13a, 13b	7.25	21.2	810	1469

11 Days

For fit walkers used to trekking. You will need to be in shape before starting as Days 1 and 2 are tough.

Day	Stages	Time (hr)	Km	Ascent (m)	Descent (m)
1	1a, 1b, 1c, 1d, 2a	8.25	24.9	1464	975
2	2b, 2c, 3	10.75	28.7	1341	2046
3	4	6.25	12.3	1665	30
4	5, 6a	8.00	17.1	1154	1153
5	6b, 7a, 7b, 7c	9.50	24.1	1143	1933
6	8	5.75	10.9	1676	518
7	9a, 9b	5.75	15.7	574	1725
8	10	6.25	16.8	1270	1126
9	11	7.25	17.1	1096	1787
10	12	7.75	17.2	1862	725
11	13a, 13b	7.25	21.2	810	1469

10 Days

These ten relentless and challenging days are for very fit walkers only. It starts hard and stays hard all the way to the end. Day 7 is a monster!

Day	Stages	Time (hr)	Km	Ascent (m)	Descent (m)
1	1a, 1b, 1c, 1d, 2a	8.25	24.9	1464	975
2	2b, 2c, 3	10.75	28.7	1341	2046
3	4	6.25	12.3	1665	30
4	5, 6a	8.00	17.1	1154	1153
5	6b, 7a, 7b, 7c	9.50	24.1	1143	1933
6	8, 9a	8.00	17.7	1772	1066
7	9b, 10	9.75	25.7	1748	2303
8	11	7.25	17.1	1096	1787
9	12	7.75	17.2	1862	725
10	13a, 13b	7.25	21.2	810	1469

Variant Stages

Stage No	Start/Finish	Time (hr)	Km	Ascent (m)	Descent (m)	Max. Altitude (m)
v1d	Col de Balme to Refuge les Grands	1.50	4.1	131	209	2203
v1e	Refuge les Grands to Col de la Forclaz	2.00	6.0	20	607	2113
v2b	Col de la Forclaz to Champex (via Bovine)	4.75	14.8	741	790	2049
v5	Cabane du Mont Fort to Cabane de Prafleuri (via Col de la Chaux)	5.75	10.6	987	781	2987
v6b	Refuge de la Gentiane to Arolla (via Cabane des Dix)	6.50	16.0	846	1295	2928
v8	La Sage to Barrage de Moiry (via Col de Torrent)	5.25	13.5	1378	672	2915
v10a	Zinal to Hotel Weisshorn	3.75	11.3	819	156	2423
v10b	Hotel Weisshorn to Gruben (via Cabane Bella-Tola)	5.50	16.0	715	1234	2789
v12a	St-Niklaus to Grächen	1.75	4.6	540	48	1619
v12b	Grächen to Europahütte	7.00	15.5	1376	731	2696
v12c	St-Niklaus to Randa (via Herbriggen)	2.50	9.6	329	47	1409
v12d	Randa to Europahütte	2.50	4.0	866	11	2264
v13	Randa to Zermatt (via Täsch)	2.75	11.1	281	85	1645

A signpost on Col des Roux (Stage 6a)

Accommodation

Zermatt lies in the shadow of the iconic Matterhorn

The WHR is a popular trek and the quality of accommodation is now excellent. In July and August, forward booking is essential and these days, many people have their entire trip booked before they depart. During that period, the days of 'seeing how you go' are things of the past. Even outside of July and August, it is wise to book ahead, particularly at weekends and on sub-stages where there is only one place to stay. In June and September, fewer people walk the route so there is less demand for accommodation: in these periods you can often still get away with only booking a day or two in advance. However, you can get caught out if, for example, a large group has booked up a lot of beds. Before mid-June, and from mid-September onwards, some accommodation may be closed so check in advance. Also, be aware that Stages 1c, 1d, 2a, 2b and 2c share the trail with the TMB so demand for accommodation is great. And the Ultra Trail du Mont Blanc (UTMB), a long distance trail running race, takes place each year in the last week of August or first week of September: during the race, accommodation around the Chamonix valley can be scarce.

The following are hot-spots where accommodation can be particularly hard to secure:

▶ **Chamonix:** during the UTMB

▶ **Col de la Forclaz:** the hotel is the only place to stay and is sometimes booked up by groups

▶ **Cabane du Mont Fort:** it is a very long way to the next hut and there is nowhere else to stay

Our favourite places to stay

1. Cabane de Moiry (Stage 8)
2. Refuge de la Gentiane (Stage 6a)
3. Relais d'Arpette (Stage 2b)
4. Hotel le Trift, Zinal (Stage 9b)
5. Cabane du Mont Fort (Stage 4)

- **Cabane de Prafleuri:** a notoriously difficult place to contact. If you cannot secure a booking, consider continuing to the unmanned Refuge de la Gentiane
- **La Sage:** there is only one gîte and a hotel
- **Cabane de Moiry:** this is a highlight of the trip so book ahead
- **Gruben:** the hotel is often booked up, particularly at weekends. It is a long way to the next accommodation
- **St-Niklaus:** surprisingly there is little accommodation in this town. If you cannot secure a booking then you may have to continue to Grächen, Herbriggen or Randa
- **Europahütte:** this is a highlight of the trip so book ahead

Full accommodation listings are provided below. All contact details were correct at the date of press but be aware that this information frequently changes. Please let us know about any changes.

Hotels:
The majority of hotels are in the one to three star categories and quality varies. Normally, they offer breakfast and evening meals and half-board can be good value. Most hotels have their own websites.

Gîtes d'étape:
Traditionally, a gîte would have been comparable to a youth hostel, offering beds in dormitories and evening meals. These days, gîtes are often more upmarket: private rooms are sometimes available and they can be better than some hotels. Most gîtes now have their own websites.

> ### Hut Etiquette
> Take off your boots before entering
>
> Tell the gardien (hut manager) that you have arrived
>
> Always use a sleeping sheet
>
> Pay before you go to bed
>
> Do not make noise after 9pm as most walkers go to bed early
>
> If you change your plans, always call to cancel your reservation to make sure someone else can take your place

Refuges/Cabanes:
These are mountain huts which offer dormitory accommodation, meals and alcohol. Refuges are often situated in the heart of the mountains where they are accessible only to the walker. A stay in a refuge can be one of the highlights of a mountain adventure such as the WHR. They are basic but they are good value: a bed, dinner and breakfast should cost around €50 in France and will be about 20% more expensive in Switzerland. If you are lucky, the gardien (manager) may let you sample some homemade Génépy, a potent liqueur made from a plant only found in the high mountains.

To stay in a refuge, you will need a sleeping sheet which is a thin bag made of silk or cotton. They can be purchased cheaply at most outdoor shops in the UK, US or France. Unlike the TMB, many of the huts on the WHR still charge for showers: we expect that this will change in the near future. Refuges are normally manned from June to September.

A typical dormitory in a refuge

Camping

The campsite at Täsch (Stage v13)

Camping on the WHR is harder than on the TMB but some still do it. Between Chamonix and Champex, it is straightforward as there are plenty of places where camping is permitted. However, after Champex campsites are scarce and in Switzerland it is rarely permitted to camp at mountain huts. A list of current official camping locations is set out below.

Wild camping is largely prohibited on the WHR. In France, around the Chamonix Valley, local laws provide that it is only permitted to bivouac 'at high altitude' from sunset to sunrise. It is not clear what 'high altitude' means exactly but presumably these rules exist to facilitate climbers and mountaineers who often sleep out on long routes. In the parts of Switzerland through which the WHR travels, we understand that wild camping is forbidden. All rules and laws are subject to change so check with the local tourist offices before setting out. If you get caught breaking the rules, you could get a stiff fine: we warned you!

You do hear of WHR walkers that wild camp by being discrete, staying high and only pitching up late in the day. But we cannot condone the breaking of rules. If you do camp wild, always take your rubbish with you (including toilet paper) and bury your toilet waste away from watercourses. Leave no trace.

Physically, camping on the WHR is a tougher option as you will need to carry more gear: tent, sleeping bag, sleeping mat, cooker, food, etc. The extra weight makes a difference to your legs over 206km. That said, there is some incredibly lightweight camping gear available these days.

Stage	Camping Location	Camping Details (Contact info is set out in the Accommodation Listings)
Start	Chamonix	Camping les Arolles
1a	Les Praz de Chamonix	Camping de la Mer de Glace
1a	Argentière	Camping du Glacier
1d	Le Peuty	Camping le Peuty beside Refuge du Peuty
2a	Col de la Forclaz	Hôtel du Col de la Forclaz. Charges apply
2b	Arpette	Camping permitted at Relais d'Arpette. Charges apply. Toilets/showers
v2b	Champex-d'en-Haut	Camping permitted at Auberge Gîte Bon Abri. Charges apply. Toilets/showers
2c/v2b	Champex	Camping les Rocailles
6b/v6b	Arolla	Camping Arolla
7b	Les Haudères	Camping Molignon
9b	Zinal	Relais de la Tzoucdana
v13	Täsch	Camping Alphubel
13b/v13	Zermatt	Camping Zermatt

The remote Turtmanntal Valley (Stage 10)

Accommodation Listings

The stunning lake at Champex (Stage 2c/v2b)

Stage No.	Accommodation	Facilities	Opening Dates	Contact Details
Chamonix	Camping les Arolles	▲	June to end Sept	+33 (0)6 75 02 26 44 infocamping@lesarolles.com www.lesarolles.com
Chamonix	Gîte Vagabond	🍴	All year	+33 (0)4 50 53 15 43 www.gitevagabond.eu
Chamonix	Chamonix Youth Hostel	🍴	May to end Sept	+33 (0)4 50 53 14 52 chamonix@hifrance.org www.hifrance.org
Chamonix	Hotel le Prieuré	🍴	All year	+33 (0)4 50 53 20 72 reservation@prieurechamonix.com www.prieurechamonix.com
Chamonix	Hôtel de l'Arve	B&B	All year	+33 (0)4 50 53 02 31 reservation@hotelarve-chamonix.com www.hotelarve-chamonix.com
1a	Camping de la Mer de Glace, les Praz de Chamonix	▲	May to end Sept	www.chamonix-camping.com
1a	Hotel Eden Chamonix, les Praz de Chamonix	12 rooms 🍴	All year	+33 (0)4 50 53 18 43 relax@hoteleden-chamonix.com www.hoteleden-chamonix.com

Stage No.	Accommodation	Facilities	Opening Dates	Contact Details
1a	Camping du Glacier d'Argentière, Argentière	▲ ♟	May to end Sept	+33 (0)4 50 54 17 36 info@campingchamonix.com www.campingchamonix.com
1a	Hôtel de la Couronne, Argentière	35 rooms ♟	All year	+33 (0)4 50 54 00 02 info@hotelcouronne.com www.hotelcouronne.com
1a	Gîte le Belvedere, Argentière	11 rooms ♟	June to end Sept	+33 (0)4 50 18 50 66 gitelebelvedere@gmail.com www.gitelebelvedere.com
1b	L'Olympique Hôtel, le Tour	13 rooms ♟	Mid-June to mid-Sept	+33 (0)4 50 54 01 04 hotel.olympique@orange.fr www.hotel-olympique-chamonix.com
1b	Chalet Alpin du Tour, le Tour	87 beds ♟	June to mid-Sept	+33 (0)4 50 54 04 16 ffcam.fr
1c	Gîte d'Alpage Les Ecuries de Charamillon	19 beds ♟	Mid-June to mid-Sept	+33 (0)4 50 54 17 07 www.les-ecuries-de-charamillon.fr
1c	Refuge du Col de Balme	20 beds ♟	End June to mid-Sept	+33 (0)4 50 54 02 33 +33 (0)6 07 06 16 30
1d	Refuge du Peuty	20 beds ♟ ▲	June to Sept	+41(0)78 719 29 83
1d (off WHR)	Auberge du Mont Blanc, Trient	126 beds ♟	All year	+41 (0)27 767 15 05 info@aubergemontblanc.com www.aubergemontblanc.com
1d (off WHR)	Hôtel La Grande Ourse, Trient	65 beds ♟	June to Sept	+41 (0)27 722 17 54 contact@la-grande-ourse.ch www.la-grande-ourse.ch
v1d	Refuge les Grands	15 beds ♟	End June to mid-Sept	Contact is difficult! +41 (0)26 660 65 04 +41 (0)26 548 13 23 +41 (0)26 662 13 33 +41 (0)79 567 19 34 clesquereux@bluewin.ch

Stage No.	Accommodation	Facilities	Opening Dates	Contact Details
2a/v1e	Hôtel du Col de la Forclaz	65 beds ¶¶ ▲	All year	+41 (0)27 722 26 88 colforclazhotel@bluewin.ch www.coldelaforclaz.ch
2b	Relais d'Arpette	100 beds ¶¶ ▲	June to Sept	+41 (0)27 783 12 21 info@arpette.ch www.arpette.ch
v2b	Auberge Gîte Bon Abri	52 beds ¶¶ ▲	June to Sept	+41 (0)27 783 14 23 contact@gite-bon-abri.com www.gite-bon-abri.com
2c/v2b	Le Cabanon, Champex	4 rooms ¶¶	Check in advance	+41 (0)27 783 11 72 www.le-cabanon.ch
2c/v2b	Hôtel Alpina, Champex	¶¶	All year	+41 (0)27 783 18 92 www.alpinachampex.ch
2c/v2b	Hôtel Splendide, Champex	25 beds ¶¶	Check in advance	+41 (0)27 783 11 45 hotel-splendide@bluemail.ch www.hotel-splendide.ch
2c/v2b	Hôtel du Glacier, Champex	¶¶	All year	+41 (0)27 782 61 51 info@hotelglacier.ch www.hotelglacier.ch
2c/v2b	Pension en Plein Air, Champex	62 beds ¶¶	Mid-June to mid-Sept	+41 (0)27 783 23 50 pensionenpleinair@gmail.com www.pensionenpleinair.ch
2c/v2b	Boulangerie-pâtisserie Tea-Room Gentiana, Champex		Check in advance	+41 (0)27 783 12 58 leonlovey@netplus.ch
2c/v2b	Camping les Rocailles, Champex	▲	All year	+41 (0)27 783 19 79 www.champex-camping.ch
3	Hotel de la Poste, le Châble	9 rooms ¶¶	All year	+41 (0)27 776 11 69 info@hotellechable.com www.hotellechable.com
3	Dzardy's Backpackers, le Châble		June to Sept	+41 (0)79 197 47 53 info@dzardys-backpacker.ch
3	Hotel le Giétroz, le Châble	14 rooms ¶¶	June to Sept	+41 (0)27 776 11 84 hoteldugietroz@netplus.ch www.hotel-gietroz.ch

Stage No.	Accommodation	Facilities	Opening Dates	Contact Details
3	Hôtel l'Escale, le Châble	🍴	All year	+41 (0)27 776 27 07 info@restaurantlescale.ch www.restaurantlescale.ch
4	Cabane du Mont Fort	58 beds 🍴	End June to mid-Sept	+41 (0)27 778 13 84 cabanemontfort@verbier.ch www.cabanemontfort.ch
5	Cabane de Prafleuri	59 beds 🍴 Hard to contact	End June to mid-Sept	+41 (0)27 281 17 80 +41 (0)79 628 46 32 +41 (0)79 939 27 75 prafleuri@bluewin.ch babeth.dayer@gmail.com
6a	Cabane les Ecoulaies	22 beds Unmanned	All year	+41 (0)79 339 12 46 andy.gaspoz@lespyramides.ch www.lespyramides.ch
6a	Refuge de la Gentiane, la Barmaz	24 beds Unmanned	All year	+41 (0)79 847 11 18 +41 (0)79 869 70 17 cabane@gym-mache.ch www.gym-mache.ch/barmaz
6b/v6b	Grand Hôtel Kurhaus, Arolla	🍴	End June to mid Sept	+41 (0)27 283 70 00 hotel-kurhaus@arolla.com www.arolla.com/kurhaus
6b/v6b	Camping Arolla, Arolla	▲	Mid-June to mid-Sept	+41 (0)27 283 22 95 www.camping-arolla.com
6b/v6b	Hôtel du Glacier, Arolla	🍴 Dormitories	All year	+41 (0)27 283 12 18 info@hotelduglacier.ch www.hotelduglacier.ch
6b/v6b	Chalet Edelweiss, Arolla	🍴 Dormitories	End June to mid Sept	+41 (0)27 283 23 12 coloedelweiss@bluewin.ch
6b/v6b	Hôtel du Mont Collon, Arolla	🍴	End June to mid Sept	+41 (0) 27 283 11 91 info@hotelmontcollon.ch www.hotelmontcollon.ch
6b/v6b	Hôtel du Pigne, Arolla	12 rooms 🍴	Mid-june to mid-Sept	+41 (0)27 283 71 00 hotel.pigne@bluewin.ch www.hoteldupigne.ch

Stage No.	Accommodation	Facilities	Opening Dates	Contact Details
6b/v6b	Chalet les Ecureuils, Arolla	🍴 dormitories	End June to mid-Sept	+41 (0)27 283 14 68 mm.fauchere@arolla.com
v6b	Cabane des Dix	120 beds 🍴	End June to end Sept	+41 (0)27 281 15 23 +41 (0)79 197 31 14 info@cabanedesdix.ch www.cabanedesdix.com
7a	Pension du Lac Bleu, la Gouille	9 rooms 🍴	Mid-June to mid-Sept	+41 (0)27 283 11 66 +33 (0)6 74 17 84 28 www.pension-du-lac-bleu.ch
7b	Camping Molignon, les Haudères	Rooms ▲ 🍴	May to Sept	+41 (0)27 283 12 40 info@molignon.ch www.camping-molignon.ch
7b	Hôtel les Haudères, les Haudères	25 rooms	End June to mid-Sept	+41(0)27 283 15 41 hoteldeshauderes@bluewin.ch www.hoteldeshauderes.ch
7b	Hôtel Dents de Veisivi, les Haudères	🍴	End June to mid-Sept	+41 (0)27 283 11 01 veisivi@bluewin.ch www.veisivi.ch
7b	Hôtel - Gîte des Alpes, les Haudères	5 rooms 🍴	Mid-June to mid-Sept	+41 (0)27 283 16 77 alpes.hauderes@bluewin.ch www.hotel-gite-alpes-hauderes.com
7b	Hotel les Mélèzes, les Haudères	🍴	June to Sept	+41 (0)27 283 11 55 info@hotelmelezes.ch www.hotelmelezes.ch
7c	Hôtel de la Sage, la Sage	🍴	June to Sept	+41 (0)27 283 24 20 hoteldelasage@bluewin.ch www.lasage-boutiquehotel.com
7c	Gîte L'Ecureuil, la Sage	30 beds 🍴	End June to mid-Sept	+41 (0)27 283 24 55
8	Cabane de Moiry	100 beds 🍴 Winter room	Mid-June to mid-Sept	Online bookings only: www.cabane-moiry.ch
v8/9a	Le Gîte de Moiry, Barrage de Moiry	24 beds 🍴	End June to mid-Sept	+41 (0)27 475 15 48 clems@netplus.ch www.moiryresto.ch/gite

Stage No.	Accommodation	Facilities	Opening Dates	Contact Details
9b	Hôtel le Trift, Zinal	🍴	June to Sept	+41 (0)27 475 14 66 www.letriftzinal.com
9b	Hôtel le Besso, Zinal	11 rooms 🍴	June to Sept	+41 (0)27 475 31 65 info@lebesso.com www.le-besso.ch
9b	Pension de la Poste, Zinal	🍴	June to Sept	+41 (0) 27 475 11 87 www.lapostezinal.ch
9b	Auberge Alpina, Zinal	6 rooms/ dormitory B&B	June to Sept	+41 (0)27 475 12 24 info@auberge-alpina.ch www.auberge-alpina.ch
9b	Relais de la Tzoucdana, Zinal	Rooms/ dormitory 🍴 ▲	Mid-June to mid-Sept	+41 (0)27 475 12 19 +41 (0)79 521 88 59 www.tzoucdana.ch/ tzoucdana.ch
10/v10b	Hotel Schwarzhorn, Gruben	15 rooms/ dormitory 🍴	June to Sept	+41 (0)27 932 14 14 info@hotelschwarzhorn.ch www.hotelschwarzhorn.ch
10/v10b	Restaurant-Pension Waldesruh, Gruben	Dormitory 🍴	End June to mid-Sept	+41 (0)79 274 62 18
v10a	Hôtel Weisshorn	🍴	June to mid-Oct	+41 (0)27 475 11 06 info@weisshorn.ch www.weisshorn.ch
v10b	Cabane Bella-Tola	92 beds 🍴	End June to mid-Sept	+41 (0)27 476 15 67 +41 (0)79 639 81 16 cabane@funiluc.ch www.cabanebellatola.ch
11	Junger-Stübli, Jungen	6 beds	End June to mid-Sept	Difficult to contact +41 (0)79 922 46 12 +41 (0)27 956 21 01
11	Hôtel la Réserve, St-Niklaus	🍴	June to Sept	+41 (0)27 955 22 55 info@la-reserve.ch www.la-reserve.ch
v12a	Hotel Alpha, Grächen	B&B	June to Sept	+41 (0)27 956 13 01 www.alpha-graechen.com
v12a	B&B Hotel Alpina, Grächen	B&B	June to Sept	+41(0)27 955 26 00 info@hotelalpinagraechen.ch www.hotelalpinagraechen.ch

Stage No.	Accommodation	Facilities	Opening Dates	Contact Details
v12a	Hotel Zum See, Grächen	🍴	June to Sept	+41 (0)27 956 24 24 info@hotel-zum-see.ch www.hotel-zum-see.ch
v12a	Hotel Eden, Grächen	20 rooms 🍴	June to Sept	+41 (0)27 956 26 66 info@eden-hotel.ch www.eden-hotel.ch
v12a	Hotel Sonne, Grächen	🍴	June to Sept	+41 (0)27 956 11 07 hotel.sonne7@bluewin.ch
12 v12b v12d	Europahütte	🍴	End June to mid-Sept	+41 (0)27 967 82 47 +41 (0)79 291 33 22 europahuette@sunrise.ch www.europahuette.ch
v12c	Hotel Bergfreund, Herbriggen	Rooms/dormitory 🍴	June to Sept	+41 (0) 27 955 23 23 info@hotel-bergfreund.ch www.hotel-bergfreund.ch
v12c	Hotel Klein Matterhorn, Randa	🍴	June to Sept	+41 (0)79 418 07 86 hotelranda@gmail.com www.hotelkleinmatterhorn.com
v12c	Matterhorn Golf Hotel, Randa	🍴	June to Sept	+41 (0)27 967 32 33 www.matterhorngolfhotel.com
13a	Europaweghütte, Täschalp	20 beds 🍴	End June to end Sept	+41 (0)27 967 23 01 kontakt@europaweghuette.ch www.europaweghuette.ch
v13	Alpine Budget Rooms, Täsch	8 beds	All year	+41 (0)27 966 62 62 info@taescherhof.ch www.taescherhof.ch
v13	Camping Alphubel, Täsch	Dormitory ▲	May to Oct	+41 (0)27 967 36 35 welcome@campingtaesch.ch www.campingtaesch.ch
13b/v13	Camping Zermatt, Zermatt	▲	Mid-June to end Sept	+41 (0)79 536 46 30 info@campingzermatt.ch www.campingzermatt.ch

Stage No.	Accommodation	Facilities	Opening Dates	Contact Details
13b/v13	Hotel Bahnhof, Zermatt	Rooms/ dormitory	All year	+41 (0)27 967 24 06 welcome@ hotelbahnhofzermatt.com www.hotelbahnhofzermatt.com
13b/v13	The Matterhorn Hostel, Zermatt	Rooms/ dormitory 🍴	All year	+41 (0)27 968 19 19 info@matterhornhostel.com www.matterhornhostel.com
13b/v13	Youth Hostel, Zermatt	Rooms/ dormitory	All year	+41 (0)27 967 23 20 zermatt@youthhostel.ch www.youthhostel.ch
13b/v13	Hotel Bristol, Zermatt	🍴	All year	+41 (0)27 966 33 66 info@hotel-bristol.ch www.hotel-bristol.ch
13b/v13	Le Petit Charme Inn, Zermatt	20 rooms B&B	All year	+41 (0)27 967 59 00 info@hotel-zermatt.com www.hotel-zermatt.com
13b/v13	Hotel Astoria, Zermatt	🍴	All year	+41 (0)27 967 52 22 astoria.zermatt@reconline.ch www.astoria-zermatt.ch

Many overlook stage v2b which is a shame as it is spectacular

Food

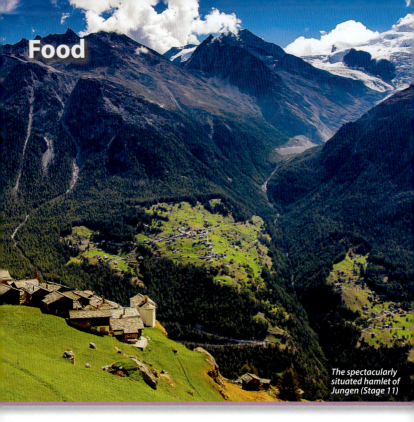

The spectacularly situated hamlet of Jungen (Stage 11)

The quality of food on the WHR is generally high. Walkers are hungry people and most accommodation caters for this providing breakfast, dinner and packed lunches for the following day. Evening meals are generally substantial three course affairs suitable for weary hikers. A starter, often soup, is normally followed by a main course of meat with vegetables, rice, pasta or salad. This will often be rounded off with dessert or cheese. Vegetarian and vegan options will normally be available on request. Breakfast varies in quality: in refuges which are off the beaten track, it is often the functional minimum of coffee, bread and jam, perhaps with some cheeses or cold meats if you are lucky. Closer to civilisation, quality tends to improve.

Local specialities are often rich and filling (and cheese based!): for example, fondues (basically melted cheese mixed with wine that you dip bread into) and tartiflette (a tasty concoction of potatoes, cream, ham and Reblochon cheese).

For lunch there are sometimes restaurants or mountain huts on route but it is generally more convenient, and cheaper, to picnic amongst the mountains. Fortunately, excellent bread is available in bakeries and supermarkets in the villages: indeed bread is nothing short of a way of life in France. And supermarkets and local shops stock a wide range of fantastic cheeses and cold meats. However, a little forward planning is required as there are some stages where there are no shops. If you get caught out then packed lunches can normally be bought from your accommodation: order them the night before. Be conscious of shop opening hours: often they will close for a long lunch (somewhere between 12 and 3pm) and then open for a few hours in the late afternoon. If you arrive in a village late then the shops may all be closed.

Facilities

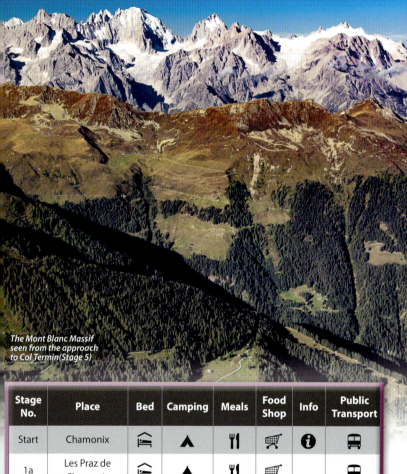

The Mont Blanc Massif seen from the approach to Col Termin (Stage 5)

Stage No.	Place	Bed	Camping	Meals	Food Shop	Info	Public Transport
Start	Chamonix	🛏	▲	🍴	🛒	ⓘ	🚌
1a	Les Praz de Chamonix	🛏	▲	🍴	🛒		🚌
1a	Chalet du Paradis			🍴			
1a	Argentière	🛏	▲	🍴	🛒	ⓘ	🚌
1b	Le Tour	🛏		🍴			
1c	Charamillon	🛏		🍴			

Stage No.	Place	Bed	Camping	Meals	Food Shop	Info	Public Transport
1c	Refuge du Col de Balme	🛏		🍴			
1d	Le Peuty	🛏	⛺	🍴			
1d	Trient (off WHR)	🛏		🍴			
v1d	Refuge les Grands	🛏		🍴			
2a/v1e	Col de la Forclaz	🛏	⛺	🍴	🛒		
2b/v1e	Chalet du Glacier			🍴			
2b	Relais d'Arpette	🛏	⛺	🍴			
v2b	Bovine			🍴			
v2b	Plan de l'Au			🍴			
v2b	Champex-d'en-Haut	🛏	⛺	🍴			
2c/v2b	Champex	🛏	⛺	🍴	🛒	ℹ	🚌
3	Le Châble	🛏		🍴	🛒		🚌
4	Cabane du Mont Fort	🛏		🍴			
5/v5	Cabane de Prafleuri	🛏		🍴			
6a	Cabane les Ecoulaies	🛏		🍴 week-end only			
6a	Refuge de la Gentiane, la Barmaz	🛏		🍴 week-end only			
v6b	Cabane des Dix	🛏		🍴			
6b/v6b	Arolla	🛏	⛺	🍴	🛒	ℹ	🚌
7a	Le Louché			🍴			

Stage No.	Place	Bed	Camping	Meals	Food Shop	Info	Public Transport
7a	La Gouille	🛏		🍴			🚌
7b	Les Haudères	🛏	▲	🍴	🛒		🚌
7c	La Sage	🛏		🍴	🛒		
8	Cabane de Moiry	🛏		🍴			
9a/v8	Barrage de Moiry Junction	🛏		🍴			
9b	Sorebois			🍴			
9b	Zinal	🛏	▲	🍴	🛒	ℹ	🚌
10/v10b	Gruben	🛏		🍴			
v10a	Hôtel Weisshorn	🛏		🍴			
v10b	Cabane Bella-Tola	🛏		🍴			
11	Jungen	🛏		🍴			
11	St-Niklaus	🛏		🍴	🛒	ℹ	🚌
v12a	Grächen	🛏		🍴	🛒	ℹ	🚌
12/v12b/v12d	Europahütte	🛏		🍴			
v12c	Randa	🛏		🍴	🛒	ℹ	🚌
13a	Täschalp	🛏		🍴			
13b	Tufteren			🍴			
13b	Sunnegga/Ze Gassu			🍴			
v13	Täsch	🛏	▲	🍴	🛒	ℹ	🚌
13/v13	Zermatt	🛏	▲	🍴	🛒	ℹ	🚌

Getting There

On Stage 5, say farewell to the Mont Blanc Massif

By air: The closest international airport to Chamonix is Geneva in Switzerland. Both Geneva and Zurich airports are accessible from Zermatt. See below for on-travel from Geneva airport.

By train: Chamonix is accessible by train from Paris Gare de Lyon with a few changes. These train services could be linked with the Eurostar from London or a flight to Paris. There are also trains from Geneva and Martigny to Champex.

By car: You could leave a car in Chamonix and get public transport back again to pick it up at the end of the trek. This would involve a train from Zermatt to Geneva and then onward transport to Chamonix (see below). It has to be said though that this would not be a cheap option. You can take a car to France by ferry from a number of different ports in Ireland or the UK. Alternatively, take a car on the train from the UK through the channel tunnel (www.eurotunnel.com). The drive from the French ports to Chamonix should take 8–9hr. From Calais or Dunkirk, the road to Reims can be preferable to avoid the busy Paris ring road.

Getting to the WHR from Geneva Airport

Minibus Transfers: This is the best way of getting to Chamonix. A number of companies offer shared and private transfers throughout the day which are scheduled to depart shortly after flights land. They must be booked in advance and take about 90min.

Bus: Scheduled buses to Chamonix run a number of times each day. Advance booking is recommended.

Train: You can travel to Chamonix by train from Geneva airport but it takes at least four hours and you will have to change two or three times. It is also expensive. One route goes via Martigny/Vallorcine and another via St-Gervais-les-Bains. To get to Champex (Stage 3), take the train from Geneva Airport to Orsières via Martigny. From there, take the bus to Champex. There are also trains from Geneva Airport to le Châble (Stage 4).

Getting home: Regular trains run from Zermatt directly to Geneva airport (4hr) or Zurich airport (3.5hr). Really, that's it!

Further information:

Minibus Transfers: www.alpybus.com; www.mountaindropoffs.com

Trains: www.sbb.ch (Switzerland); www.en.oui.sncf (France)

Buses: www.gare-routiere.com (France); www.sbb.ch (Switzerland)

Ferries: www.stenaline.co.uk; www.irishferries.com; www.brittany-ferries.co.uk; www.dfdsseaways.co.uk

The Aiguilles Rouges tower above the village of le Tour (Stage 1b)

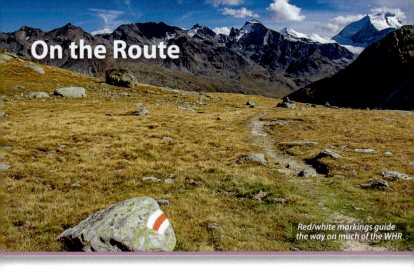

On the Route

Red/white markings guide the way on much of the WHR

Costs

As vacations go, long-distance walking in Europe is relatively inexpensive: walking itself is free! No permits are required. In French refuges and gîtes, breakfast, dinner and a bed normally costs around €50. In Switzerland, such costs are a little higher: perhaps 70-90 Swiss Francs. Hotels cost a bit more. Packed lunches cost €9-10. If you camp and/or cook for yourself, then you could get by on €30 each day.

Weather

The Alps have a relatively dry and predictable climate compared to mountains in the UK or the US west coast. However, conditions can still change quickly so be prepared for rain. Furthermore, snow is always possible on cols and summits, even in the middle of summer. Mountains can be dangerous so treat them with respect and caution, even if the weather forecast is favourable.

The region has a number of micro-climates with the weather often differing from valley to valley. It is possible therefore to find blazing sunshine on one side of a col and cloud or rain over the other side.

Meteo France and Meteo Swiss, the French and Swiss meteorological offices, provide national, regional and local forecasts at www.meteofrance.com and www.meteoswiss.admin.ch. They both also provide, free of charge, excellent smartphone apps which provide regularly updated local forecasts. Local forecasts are also displayed at tourist information offices and refuges. Or ask the refuge managers whose local knowledge of weather (and indeed other matters) is often invaluable.

Maps

In this book, we have included the best maps available. Each sub-stage (except for Stages 1a, 1b, 1c, 1d, v1d, v1e, 2a, 2b, v2b and 2c) has its own map produced from the official 1:50,000 scale maps made by SwissTopo, the Swiss mapping agency. Stages 1a, 1b, 1c, 1d, v1d, v1e, 2a, 2b, v2b and 2c use 1:25,000 scale maps made by IGN, the French mapping agency. Occasionally, a map has been reduced slightly to fit on the page. Although these maps normally enable you to navigate, a sheet map can be helpful, particularly in bad weather. Also, with a sheet map you get a better feel for the geography of the region as it helps you to identify peaks and landmarks sighted along the way.

Stages 1a, 1b, 1c, 1d, v1d, v1e, 2a, 2b, v2b and 2c are covered on a single 1:25,000 sheet: IGN 3630OT Chamonix-Mont-Blanc. Those who have previously walked the TMB may already have that map. However, for the remainder of the route, there is really only 1:50,000 coverage. So, perhaps the best sheet map option is to use the two 1:50,000 maps which cover the entire WHR: SwissTopo sheets 5027T (Grand St-Bernard-Combins-Arolla) and 5028T (Monte Rosa-Matterhorn).

Alternatively, Kümmerly + Frey have three 1:60,000 sheets which cover the entire WHR: Sheets 22 (Grand-St-Bernard-Dents du Midi), 23 (Val d'Anniviers-Val d'Hèrens) and 24 (Zermatt-Saas Fee).

However, perhaps the best overall solution is to combine this book with a smart phone app: SwissTopo's fantastic app covers the entire WHR including the French sections (www.swisstopo.ch/smm). And IGN's app provides 1:25,000 maps for the French sections. Both use GPS to show your location on the map.

Paths and Waymarking

Much of the WHR uses clear paths which are easy to follow. And there are often waymarks (painted on trees and rocks) and signs to assist. Navigation in good conditions is therefore generally straightforward. However, there are some sections of the route where the trail disappears over rocks and boulders: navigation here can be more difficult, particularly in bad conditions, and you must concentrate on following the waymarks. Also, you should watch your footing carefully when walking over the rocks and boulders.

Route finding is difficult on the following sections:

- **Stage 2b:** challenging boulders on either side of Fenêtre d'Arpette

- **Stage 4:** navigation is fiddly throughout the stage due to the labyrinth of paths and tracks around the ski resort of Verbier

- **Stage 5:** a wild part of the WHR with long sections of rocks and boulders

- **Stage 6b:** the route is rocky and challenging from Lac des Dix all the way to Col de Riedmatten. Navigation would be difficult in low visibility. The section before the col would be dangerous after rain

- **Stage 8 and 9a:** the final climb to, and the descent from, Cabane de Moiry is steep and rocky

- **Stage 11:** there is a long section of boulders to cross after the Augstbordpass

- **Stages 12, 13a and 13b:** the Europaweg is as tough as it is beautiful. It is not a place to be in bad weather

In France, waymarks are usually red/white stripes. In Switzerland, there are either red/white stripes or yellow/black diamonds. Waymarking varies in quality and is at the mercy of the environment: markings can fade or be obscured by rockfalls and landslides. There are also regular signposts. Those who have completed the TMB will be accustomed to following the signs and waymarks with the "TMB" brand on them. However, on the WHR, signs and waymarks do not refer to the WHR itself: rather, they simply direct you to the next place on the map. It is up to you to work out which signpost to follow but this is normally straightforward.

As a rule of thumb, generally keep on a path unless told otherwise. A red and white cross on a rock or a tree may indicate that you are off the WHR route. Often, signposts give time or distance to a specific destination: the timings are not always reliable.

If you see mountain biking signs, usually indicated by the letters 'VTT' (Vélo Tout Terrain), then take care: mountain bikes are fast and often quiet and a collision between a walker and a mountain bike could be serious.

Water

Drinking water in the Alps is the subject of regular debate. Save in very dry seasons or towards the end of September, water is usually plentiful in rivers and streams. There are also fountains in most towns and villages and at refuges. Many walkers regularly drink untreated water from these sources without any issues. However, others insist upon filtering or treating the water first to minimise the risk of contaminants. You will have to weigh up the risks and make up your own mind. If, like many, you do decide to drink the water untreated, there are a few rules that you should follow to reduce any risk:

- Avoid water where there is evidence nearby of animals, especially cows or sheep: dead carcasses or faeces can cause contamination
- Do not collect water downstream from buildings or grazing areas
- Only drink from moving water. The faster the better
- The bigger the river/stream the better
- Generally the higher the altitude the better

If you do wish to treat your water, this can be done by way of portable filters or purification chemicals. The effectiveness of the different products and methods varies and is beyond the scope of this guide so do your research before your trip.

Also remember that availability of water at fountains and streams may vary depending upon the season: generally water courses are fullest in June and decline throughout the walking season. It is good practice to fill your water bottles each day before leaving your accommodation. Start with at least 1.5 litres per person.

Escape Routes

The WHR has many exit points with road access, enabling a walker to leave the route early, but the availability of public transport at these locations varies (see Facilities). During stages, escape would sometimes be difficult and, once started, you are committed.

Pastous

The WHR passes through rural areas and sheep and cows are grazed in the high mountains in summer. Some shepherds live at high altitude in a tiny cabin throughout the grazing season. To protect sheep from wolves (which are now present again in some parts of the Alps) and lynx, a flock sometimes has a dog to accompany it. Often, the dog is a Pastou (or Patou) which is very large, white and long-haired and is related to an old Pyrenean breed.

They are usually raised with the flock so form a close bond with the sheep: they growl or bark if you approach the flock. Although uncommon, occasionally visitors to the Alps are bitten by a Pastou which thought that there was a threat to its sheep. Accordingly, the best advice is to give them a wide berth and assume that there may be a Pastou with any flock. Remember that from afar, the colour and texture of Pastous' coats makes them hard to spot amongst the sheep. Fortunately, Pastous are less common on the WHR than on some other Alpine treks.

A Pastou keeps watch high up in the Alps

What to take

When undertaking a long-distance route in the Alps, be properly equipped for the worst terrain and the worst weather conditions which you could encounter: rain, cold and possibly snow. Being cold and wet at high altitude is unpleasant and can be dangerous. However, the dilemma is that you should also consider weight and avoid carrying anything unnecessary. The heavier your pack, the harder the climbs will be. It is perfectly possible to get by with a pack of 7kg (excluding water) yet most hikers' packs weigh much more. Be ruthless as every gram counts.

Fortunately, modern gear helps with this dilemma: there is some fantastic lightweight kit available now. For example, I recently upgraded a backpack, obtaining a weight saving of 600g (almost 10% of overall pack-weight). When choosing gear, check the weights of the different products as the differences can be great.

Layering of clothing is the key to warmth. Do not wear cotton: it does not dry quickly and gets cold. Modern walking clothes are light so make sure you have a spare set to change into if you get wet.

Recommended Basic Kit

Boots/Shoes	Good quality, properly fitting and worn in. It is fashionable these days to trek with trail running shoes but we prefer boots with ankle support and cleated soles (such as Vibram).
Socks	3 pairs of good quality, quick drying walking socks: wash one, wear one, spare one. Wash them regularly and change them daily, helping to avoid blisters.
Waterproof jacket and trousers	Waterproof and breathable. Some people do not bother with waterproof trousers but we like to carry light ones just in case.
Base layers	3 T-shirts and pants of man-made fabrics or merino wool which wick moisture away from your body: wash one, wear one, spare one.
Fleeces	2 fleeces. Man–made fabrics. Wear one, spare one.
Trousers	2 pairs of walking trousers. Wear one, spare one. Convertible ones are practical as you can remove the legs on warm days.
Warm hat and gloves	Even in summer it can be cold at altitude, especially in the evening and early morning.
Down jacket	Even in summer it can be cold at altitude, especially in the evening and early morning.
Rucksack	Get a light one. 35-45 litres should be sufficient unless you are camping. Well padded shoulder straps and waist band. Much of the weight of the pack should sit on your hips rather than your shoulders.
Waterproof Pack Liner	Rucksacks are not very waterproof. A liner will keep your spare clothes dry.
Head-torch with spare batteries	For emergencies. And you may need it in some refuges after lights out.
Whistle	For emergencies. Many rucksacks have one incorporated into the sternum strap.
Basic first aid kit	Including plasters, a bandage and antiseptic wipes.
Map and compass	For maps see above. A GPS unit or smartphone apps can be a useful addition but they are no substitute for a map and compass: after all, batteries can run out and electronics can fail.
Knife	Such as a Swiss army knife. You are going to need to cut that cheese!

Sunglasses, sun hat, sunscreen and lip salve	Sun at altitude can be brutal.
Walking poles	These transfer weight from your legs onto your arms keeping you fresher. They also save your knees, particularly on descents and can reduce the likelihood of falling or twisting an ankle.
Phone and charger (with EU adapter)	A smart phone is a very useful tool on a trek. It can be used for emergencies and apps for weather, mapping and hotel booking are invaluable. It can also replace your camera to save weight.
Towel	Lightweight trekking towel. Refuges and gîtes do not provide towels.
Shower gel	A small hotel size bottle should be enough to last the journey, saving a lot of weight.
Ziplock plastic bag	A lightweight way of keeping money, passport and credit cards dry.
Sleeping sheet	A thin bag made of silk or cotton. Required to sleep in refuges.
Ear plugs	You will thank us when someone in your dormitory snores.
Space blanket or emergency bag	Very light but it could save your life.
Food	Carry some emergency food over and above your planned daily ration. Energy bars, nuts and dried fruit are all good.
Water	Start each day with at least 1.5 litres of water per person. Hydration packs with tubes facilitate more effective hydration by enabling drinking on the move. Bring a filter or purification tablets if required.

Paragliding above Zermatt

Descending from the Augstbordpass (Stage 11)

Safety

On a calm summer's day the Alps are paradise. But a sudden weather shift or an injury can change things dramatically so treat the mountains with respect and be conscious of your experience levels and physical capabilities. The following is a non-exhaustive list of recommendations:

* The fitter you are at the start of your trip, the more you will enjoy the walking
* Before you set out each day, study the route and make plans based upon the abilities of the weakest member of your party
* Get a weather forecast (daily if possible) and reassess your plans in light of it. Avoid exposed routes if the weather is uncertain
* Start early to avoid ascending during the hottest part of the day and to allow more surplus time in case something goes wrong
* Bring a map and compass and know how to use them
* It can be sensible to call ahead to your accommodation and tell them what time you will arrive. If you do not turn up then they can raise the alarm
* Carry surplus food and clothing for emergencies
* Never be too proud to turn back if you find the going too tough or if the weather deteriorates
* Do not stray from the route so as to avoid getting lost and to help prevent erosion of the landscape
* Avoid exposed high ground in a thunderstorm. If you get caught out in one then drop your walking poles and stay away from trees, overhanging rocks, metal structures and caves. Generally accepted advice is to squat on your pack and keep as low as possible
* In the event of an accident, move an injured person into a safe place and administer any necessary first aid. Keep the victim warm. Establish your exact coordinates and, if possible, use your cell phone to call for help. The emergency numbers are set out on page 1. If you have no signal then send someone for help
* Mountain biking is now very popular in the Alps so watch out. A collision with a bike would not be pleasant

The Matterhorn reflected in Riffelsee on the day walk from Gornergrat to Riffelalp (see Zermatt Day Walks)

General Information

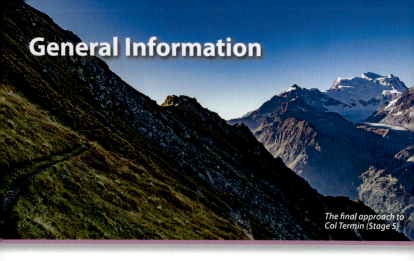

The final approach to Col Termin (Stage 5)

Language: French is the first language in France and the Valais canton of Switzerland (which the WHR traverses). However, after crossing the Forcletta or the Meidpass on Stages 10 or v10b, you enter German speaking Switzerland. In most places, locals will have at least some basic English. On the trail these days, it seems that English has been adopted as the common language of the WHR and walkers often pass each other with a greeting of 'hello'. However, when in another country, it is good manners to make an effort to say hello in that country's language. If you do so, then you will get a much more positive and friendly response from locals both on the trail and off it. You will quickly determine whether to switch to English or not.

Charging electronic devices: These days, you can charge devices at most WHR accommodation. However, at mountain huts it is not wise to assume that this will always be the case. Continental 2 pin plugs are required in France. In Switzerland, a 3-pin plug is traditional but these days some Swiss WHR accommodation provides 2-pin sockets as well. Although you can get away with just a 2-pin charger on the TMB, we find that a 3-pin one is still often required on the WHR.

Money: France uses the Euro(€). Switzerland has the Swiss Franc (CHF) but Euros are normally accepted too. On the route, there are ATMs in Chamonix, Argentière, Champex, le Châble, Zinal, St-Niklaus, Grächen and Zermatt. However, it is wise to carry surplus cash in case an ATM is out of order. Credit cards are accepted widely although most huts accept cash only.

Visas: Citizens of the European Union do not need a visa. Currently, citizens of Australia, New Zealand, Canada and the US do not need a visa for stays of up to three months. Brexit may change things for UK citizens but at the time of writing the situation is unclear.

Cell phones: There is cell phone reception almost everywhere on the WHR. However, do not rely on it absolutely. 3G/4G services are widely available so access to the internet from smart phones is normally possible.

International dialling codes: The country codes for France and Switzerland are +33 and +41 respectively. If dialling from overseas, the first 0 in French and Swiss area codes is omitted.

Wifi: Nearly all hotels and gîtes on the WHR now have wifi. Refuges/cabanes do not.

Insurance: Mountain rescue services may not be free and therefore it is wise to have adequate insurance which covers hiking. Visitors from the UK should also make sure that they have the free European Health Insurance Card (EHIC) but remember that often this will only cover part of your medical treatment so insurance is still recommended. Also, the EHIC will not cover any rescue itself. With Brexit looming it is possible that the EHIC card may soon be a thing of the past for UK residents and in such circumstances private insurance will become even more important.

The consistently exceptional Europaweg (Stage 13a)

Wildlife

Ibex are often seen in herds

Early morning is the best time for seeing wildlife. Often the first party on the trail may see many Chamois or Bouquetin but following groups will not see any.

Bouquetin (or Ibex): A member of the goat family with long scimitar shaped horns. It was saved from extinction by the Savoy kings who banned most hunting in 1821 and created a royal reserve in 1856 (which finally became Italy's Gran Paradiso National Park). After a series of reintroductions in the 20th century, they are now fairly widespread throughout the Alps.

Chamois: Another type of mountain goat which is smaller than the Bouquetin and is widespread in the regions of the WHR. It has shorter horns which do not have deep ridges. Chamois are frequently spotted in herds. They are much more wary of humans than Bouquetins.

Deer: Various species are common below the tree line. Chevreuil (Roe Deer) are reddish or grey-brown and Daim (Fallow Deer) tend to be brown with white spots. Look out for them in forests early in the morning.

Marmots: Everyone loves these fat rodents which are easily spotted in summer when they graze relentlessly to put on layers of fat to last the long winter hibernation. They live in colonies in grassy parts of the mountains, often standing upright on their hind legs like a meerkat. They whistle as you approach to warn their colony of an intruder.

Marmots are plentiful!

Sanglier (Wild Boar): A member of the pig family with small tusks. They are common in forests but hard to spot. In the unlikely event that you see one, keep your distance because they can be dangerous.

Wolves: Hunted to extinction in France in the 1930s. In recent decades, conservation efforts in Italy increased their numbers and many have now crossed the border into France through the mountains. They are protected but their presence is controversial and particularly unpopular with shepherds who lose many sheep to them. They are more common in the Alps further south, where they are occasionally spotted by walkers.

Other mammals: Squirrels, foxes, badgers and mice are fairly common below the tree line.

Fish: species of trout are found in rivers, streams and lakes. Some high alpine lakes also contain Arctic Char.

Lagopède (or Ptarmigan): A grouse-like bird. Its plumage is white in the winter and largely brown in the summer.

Golden Eagle: (pictured left) During the hot parts of the day they can sometimes be seen circling in the thermals to gain altitude as they scan the ground for prey.

Gypaète Barbu (or Bearded Vulture): A vulture with a wingspan of up to 3m. In Germany it was given the name 'Lammergeier' ('lamb-hawk') because it was believed that it attacked lambs. They are rare and you are more likely to spot one in the Alps further south.

Ibex have special hooves enabling them to traverse steep rock faces

Flowers

Alpenrose carpet the slopes in early summer

The Alps are home to thousands of plant species including the incredible wild-flowers. June is a fabulous month for flowers, which wait patiently throughout the winter for the snow to clear and then rapidly spring to life. At this time, carpets of different colours cover the slopes and pastures. Although spring is the peak time for flowers, there are still plenty throughout the summer. Watch out for the following:

Alpenrose: A bright pink member of the Rhododendron family which coats the slopes at altitude in June/July.

Viola: A small flower in a variety of colours including yellow, white and blue (or a combination of those colours). It is often found in grassy areas.

Edelweiss: It may be the most famous alpine plant, perhaps because it has a song named after it. This rare white flower is striking and hard to spot because it only grows at high altitude (1800–3300m).

Route Summary

The WHR skirts the edge of Lac des Dix (Stage 6b)

Stage	Start	Summary
1a	Chamonix	The WHR begins with a straightforward climb out of Chamonix and up the Vallée de l'Arve to the attractive town of Argentière. The first half of the stage leads through Chamonix's outlying settlements on roads and paths. The jagged towers of les Drus will keep you company but it is a relief to climb into the forest after les Praz de Chamonix. Then an undulating path leads to Argentière which has shops and places to stay.
1b	Argentière	This is a short stage but the scenery gets more beautiful as you continue up the Chamonix Valley. Climb steeply out of Argentière into forest. As you get higher, gaps in the trees offer fabulous views of the Aiguilles Rouges to the W. And soon the lovely hamlet of le Tour comes into view below.
1c	Le Tour	This is where the WHR notches up a level. The gradient increases and, at last, you climb out of the valley and into the high mountains. Quickly, the views open up with the whole of the Chamonix Valley and the MB Massif behind you: for the first time on the trek, the scenery will take your breath away. After a long climb, reach the first col of the WHR: Col de Balme. The views are exquisite.
1d	Col de Balme	The first stage on Swiss territory involves a long descent from Col de Balme to the pretty hamlet of le Peuty: really nothing more than a few buildings set amongst grassy pastures which are littered with wildflowers in early summer.

Stage	Start	Summary
v1d/ v1e	Refuge les Grands Variant	The variant is scenically superior to the main WHR (Stages 1d and 2a). In particular, Stage v1d is wonderful. The views of Glacier du Trient are beautiful and Refuge les Grands is superbly situated. Beauty comes at a price here though as Stages v1d and v1e are harder than the main WHR.
2a	Le Peuty	A short climb through forest to Col de la Forclaz.
2b	Col de la Forclaz	Fenêtre d'Arpette (2665m) is a highlight of the WHR. Pray for a clear day as the view of the Glacier du Trient is exceptional. This is one of the most challenging sections of the WHR and should not be underestimated.
v2b	Bovine Variant	Climb through aromatic forest with tantalising glimpses of high peaks between the trees. Emerge from the forest at the stunning pastures around Bovine and enjoy sublime views of the Rhône Valley stretching out towards the E. Shortly afterwards, descend steeply as you head towards Champex.
2c	Arpette	A short, pretty stage involving a simple descent into the stunning lakeside town of Champex-Lac.
3	Champex	On this transition stage, travel away from the MB Massif towards the Combin Massif. It is a valley walk which is far removed from the previous high mountain stages and those to come. This part of Switzerland is gentle and green: forests of larch and pine and bucolic, flower filled pastures. And dotted around are neat and tidy chalets. A long but easy descent to the town of Sembrancher is followed by a short, gentle climb to le Châble.
4	Le Châble	A relentless and long climb through the forests around Verbier keeps you occupied for much of the day. Fortunately, the excellent views help to take your mind off the exertion. Finally, the route rises above the trees and you are treated to the spectacular sight of the Grand Combin to the SE. A superb balcony path contours around the slopes all the way to Cabane du Mont Fort: a wonderful setting for an overnight stop.
5	Cabane du Mont Fort	A highlight of the WHR, entering remote terrain and crossing three wonderful cols. First, climb to Col Termin, enjoying the WHR's last great views of the MB Massif. The following section is an incredible remote landscape of grassy slopes and snowy peaks. Soon climb the rocky Col de Louvie where both Grand Combin and Mont Blanc are visible. Next enter a remote moonscape of boulders and glacial lakes. Eventually, climb steeply to Col de Prafleuri. Then descend to Cabane de Prafleuri, set on an outcrop overlooking a barren cirque and surrounded by peaks.

Stage	Start	Summary
v5	Col de la Chaux Variant	This variant shortens Stage 5 by avoiding the detour to Col Termin and taking a more direct route straight over Col de la Chaux. Rejoin the main WHR route before Col de Louvie and follow it all the way to Cabane de Prafleuri (see above). Although, the route over Col de la Chaux is a fine walk in its own right, we still prefer Stage 5. It is, however, useful if you are short of time.
6a	Cabane de Prafleuri	A short climb out of the barren terrain surrounding Cabane de Prafleuri leads to Col des Roux where you are met by an entirely new, and starkly contrasting, vista: grassy slopes, snowy peaks, glaciers and the incredible Lac des Dix. The colour of the lake is other-worldly and the descent to Refuge de la Gentiane is Alpine walking at its finest. The normally unmanned refuge makes for one of the best overnight stops on the WHR.
6b	Refuge de la Gentiane, la Barmaz	An easy stroll beside the spectacular Lac des Dix leads to possibly the most challenging section of the WHR. Head up into a barren but stunning glacial valley dominated by the peak of Mont Blanc de Cheilon. Then, climb very steeply up the E flank of the valley to Col de Riedmatten. A long descent follows all the way to the lovely village of Arolla.
v6b	Cabane des Dix Variant	This fantastic variant enables you to stay at Cabane des Dix, magnificently situated next to Mont Blanc de Cheilon and the Glacier de Cheilon. Like Stage 6b, this stage involves possibly the most challenging section of the WHR. The route is shared with Stage 6b all the way up into the barren glacial valley. But then, instead of following Stage 6b up the valley floor, head up a fabulous ridge all the way to the cabane. Then after a tough moraine crossing meet up with Stage 6b again.
7a	Arolla	A short and underrated section of the WHR. Climb to the stunning Lac Bleu, with its clear blue waters. Then, descend past le Louché, a lovely hamlet which has a little buvette where you can buy local cheese. Finish at the charming hotel/restaurant at la Gouille.
7b	La Gouille	A short, scenic valley walk, descending all the way to the historical village of les Haudères with its immaculately preserved Valaisian barns and houses.
7c	Les Haudères	Another short stage which climbs to the hamlet of la Sage, a lovely place to relax for the night.
8	La Sage	The day begins with one of the WHR's longest climbs: a hefty 1676m of ascent. Fortunately, you can expect more spectacular views. The highlight of the stage is a stay at the utterly fabulous Cabane de Moiry, set right beside the Glacier de Moiry.

Stage	Start	Summary
v8	Col de Torrent Variant	A spectacular alternative to Stage 8. The vista from Col de Torrent is arguably superior to that at Col du Tsaté: the startlingly turquoise Lac de Moiry is just below to the E. The climb, up through pasture, is another big one but the views are excellent. However, the highlight is the sublime descent to Barrage de Moiry which is one of our favourite sections of the entire WHR.
9a	Cabane de Moiry	Descend from Cabane de Moiry enjoying a different perspective of the Glacier de Moiry as it basks in the low light of sunrise. Soon, head N on a superb balcony, high above the unforgettable, turquoise coloured, Lac de Moiry. On a fine day this is another highlight of the WHR.
9b	Barrage de Moiry Junction	Start with a steep climb to a saddle near Col de Sorebois: there are more fantastic views of Lac de Moiry all the way up. At the saddle you are greeted by another incredible vista which is dominated by the Weisshorn. Descend steeply through ski infrastructure to the small ski station of Sorebois. Afterwards, leave the ski fields behind as you descend very steeply through beautiful pastures and forest to Zinal on the valley floor.
10	Zinal	A long ascent out of the Val d'Anniviers to Col de la Forcletta is followed by a long descent into the Turtmanntal Valley. The views from the col are exceptional (as usual).
v10a/ v10b	Hôtel Weisshorn/ Meidpass Variant	The section of path from Zinal to Hôtel Weisshorn is one of the finest on the WHR. After a climb out of Zinal, continue on an amazing balcony path all the way to Hôtel Weisshorn. Then climb to Cabane Bella-Tola enjoying wide open views of the valley below. Afterwards, enter some of the most remote and beautiful terrain on the WHR. Pass the wonderful Lac de l'Armina (spectacularly set in a beautiful grassy cirque surrounded by peaks) and then climb to the awesome Meidpass. Finally, descend through a wilderness of tarns and grassy slopes overlooked by snowy summits.
11	Gruben	On this exceptional stage, climb out of the Turtmanntal Valley and over the Augstbordpass, the final col on the WHR. Then descend into the Mattertal Valley which will lead you triumphantly into Zermatt in a few days' time. The scenery throughout is fabulous.
12	St-Niklaus	The first section of the tough Europaweg is a clear highlight of the WHR. It is a high altitude balcony path heading S down the Mattertal Valley in the shadow of a large array of famous Swiss peaks and glaciers. It is breathtaking but walking this path carries risk so read the warnings before setting out.

Stage	Start	Summary
v12a/ v12b	Grächen Variant	A pleasant climb to the relaxing village of Grächen. From there, make your way to Gasenried where you join the route of Stage 12 (see above).
v12c	Valley Variant to Randa	This valley walk is useful if the Stage 12 section of the Europaweg is closed, the weather is bad or you are short of time. The walk is pleasant but an anti-climax after the trekking enjoyed over the previous days. Nevertheless, after Mattsand, there are superb views of the Breithorn.
v12d	Randa- Europaweg Link Variant	This stage links Randa to the Europaweg. It can be used if the Stage 12 part of the Europaweg was closed but the Stage 13a/13b sections remain open. Climb to the Charles Kuonen Suspension Bridge and then pass onto Stage 13a. Alternatively, you could use Stage v12d to climb to the Europahütte, overnight there and then walk Stages 13a and 13b the following day.
13a	Europahütte	The Europaweg continues and there are more fabulous views. However, the Matterhorn (4478m) will soon command much of your attention. Pray for good weather as these are the scenes that you have been dreaming about since Chamonix.
13b	Täschalp	The non-stop views of the Matterhorn provide a wonderful climax to the WHR. This is what you came to see and the quality of the views is in no way exaggerated. After a long and magnificent balcony path, make the long descent into Zermatt to complete the WHR.
v13	Valley Variant to Zermatt	Another valley walk which is useful if the Stage 13a/13b section of the Europaweg is closed, the weather is bad or you are short of time. This stage is more enjoyable than Stage v12c (St-Niklaus to Randa).

Cows grazing near Sorebois (Stage 9b)

Hiking close to Zermatt in the shadow of the Matterhorn

Route Description

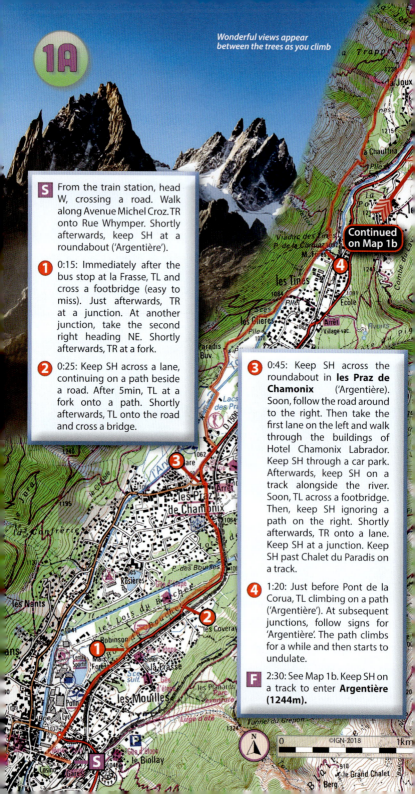

Chamonix to Argentière

1A

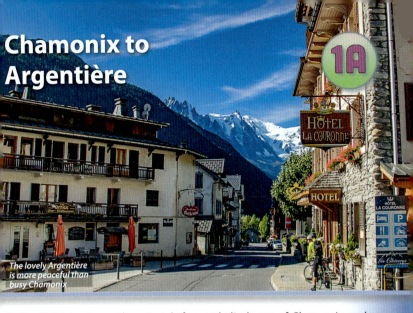

The lovely Argentière is more peaceful than busy Chamonix

The WHR begins with a straightforward climb out of Chamonix and up the Vallée de l'Arve to the attractive town of Argentière. The first half of the stage leads through Chamonix's outlying settlements on roads and paths. The jagged towers of les Drus will keep you company but it is a relief to climb into the forest after les Praz de Chamonix. Then an undulating path leads to Argentière which has shops and places to stay.

Although this stage is short, it is useful for these arriving in Chamonix late in the afternoon: you could walk straight to Argentière and overnight there. This gives your legs a good warm up for the more serious endeavours to come. Alternatively, you could skip the stage by taking the train to Argentière.

Time	2:30
Distance	9.3
Ascent	274
Descent	67
Maximum Altitude	1252
Refreshments on route	Chalet du Paradis (1:00) Argentière
Accommodation	Argentière

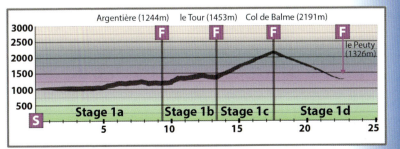

1B

Time	1:15
Distance	4.0
Ascent	252
Descent	43
Maximum Altitude	1475
Refreshments on route	Le Tour
Accommodation	Le Tour

Continued from Map 1a

The first major climb of the WHR begins after le Tour

Argentière to le Tour

1B

Les Aiguilles Rouge as seen from above le Tour

This is a short stage but the scenery gets more beautiful as you continue up the Chamonix Valley. Climb steeply out of Argentière into forest, now on the E side of the valley. As you get higher, gaps in the trees offer fabulous views of the Aiguilles Rouges to the W. And soon the lovely hamlet of le Tour comes into view below.

- **S** From the centre of Argentière, head E on Route du Village. Cross the river and after a few minutes, TR at a junction onto Chemin de la Moraine. Soon, pass under a bridge and keep SH on a track. Shortly afterwards, keep SH at a junction ('le Tour'). At the next junction, TL ('Sentier Piétons'). Shortly afterwards, TL at another junction ('le Tour').
- **1** 0:30: Keep SH at a junction ('le Tour'). At the next two junctions, keep SH ('le Tour'). Descend gently, cross a bridge and keep SH on a path.
- **2** 1:10: Pass a gîte as you enter **le Tour (1453m)**. Keep SH.
- **F** 1:15: Soon, arrive at the main road. TR and reach a restaurant and a hotel.

57

Walkers climbing from le Tour towards Col de Balme

Le Tour to Col de Balme

1C

Mont Blanc seen from le Tour

This is where the WHR notches up a level. The gradient increases and, at last, you climb out of the valley and into the high mountains. Quickly, the views open up with the whole of the Chamonix Valley and the MB Massif behind you. For the first time on the trek, the scenery will take your breath away. It will not be the last time!

After a long climb, reach the first col of the WHR: Col de Balme. The views are exquisite and it is a great setting for the refuge which was apparently built in 1877 and was occupied by German troops during World War 2. The refuge has perhaps seen better days but it is located usefully on the WHR. In front of the refuge there is a much photographed stone marker indicating the Switzerland/France frontier: this is the first and only border crossing on the WHR.

Time	2:00
Distance	4.3
Ascent	738
Descent	0
Maximum Altitude	2191
Refreshments on route	Charamillon-Balme (1:00) Col de Balme
Accommodation	Charamillon-Balme (1:00) Col de Balme

To save time (and your legs), you could use the Charamillon-Balme and/or Autannes ski lifts to ascend all or part of the way from le Tour to the col (see www.chamonix.net for opening dates/times).

> **S** Pass to the right of the **Charamillon** cable car station and climb on a track ('Col de Balme').
>
> **1** 0:20: TR onto a path ('Sentier Piétons').
>
> **2** 1:00: Keep SH at a track. Soon afterwards, TL at a cable car station. Just afterwards, TL at a fork ('Col de Balme'). A few minutes later, TL at a fork. Soon afterwards, TR on a path, climbing quite steeply. At the next junction, TL ('Col de Balme').
>
> **3** 1:55: Keep SH at a crossroads.
>
> **F** 2:00: Arrive at **Refuge du Col de Balme (2191m)**.

Col de Balme to Le Peuty

Refuge du Col de Balme

The first stage on Swiss territory involves a long descent from Col de Balme to the pretty hamlet of le Peuty: really nothing more than a few buildings set amongst grassy pastures which are littered with wildflowers in early summer. The refuge is a fantastic option especially if you could not secure a place at Hôtel du Col de la Forclaz (Stage 2a). There are other accommodation options just off the WHR in nearby Trient (directions below).

> **S** Head NE from the refuge, descending the right flank of the Nant Noir Valley. At any junctions, keep descending generally NE.
>
> **1** 1:35: Ford a river on rocks: take care in early season when there is a lot of water. After a few minutes, keep SH at a junction.
>
> **F** 1:45: Arrive at **le Peuty (1326m)**. To go to Trient for accommodation, head N from le Peuty on the road for 10min. To continue on the WHR from Trient, follow signs to Col de la Forclaz.

l'Aiguillette des Posettes seen from Col de Balme

61

Stage v1d offers the best views of Refuge du Col de Balme

V1D

Time	1:30
Distance	4.1
Ascent	131
Descent	209
Maximum Altitude	2203
Refreshments on route	Refuge les Grands
Accommodation	Refuge les Grands

Col de Balme to Refuge les Grands

V1D

Glacier du Trient seen from Stage v1d

The variant route to Col de la Forclaz described in this stage and Stage v1e is scenically superior to the main WHR (Stages 1d and 2a). Stage v1d in particular is exquisite, taking place on a magnificent balcony path: the views of Glacier du Trient and Glacier des Grands are sublime. The slopes are covered with Alpenrose and Myrtille. The route is quiet, with most people opting to stay on the main route, and so is a good place to escape the crowds.

Be warned though: the balcony path is harder than it appears on paper. It undulates relentlessly and the altitude gain and loss are significant. It is often rocky and uneven making it tiring. And it is narrow and the drops are steep so take care. There are a few sections of rocks to clamber over: follow red/white waymarks. A few steeper sections are protected with chains.

Refuge les Grands is superbly situated looking out over the valley below. Reservation is essential but the refuge is difficult to contact. There is also a winter room in the bergerie next door (where you could stay without reservation) but it is very basic. At the time of writing, it had been vandalised and was not in good condition. You would need to be equipped with a sleeping bag, mat and cooking equipment to stay in the winter room.

S See Map 1d. From the refuge, cross into Switzerland and head E on a path ('les Grands'). The path contours around the hillside with magnificent views of the Swiss Alps to the N. Soon the path gets rougher and there are short sections of rocks to cross.

1 0:35: Bear right, contouring around the hillside, generally SE. After 30min, incredible views of Glacier du Trient suddenly appear: wow!

2 1:10: The path gradually bends right and heads SW. This section is the most challenging.

F 1:30: Descend some steep rocks using a chain. Shortly afterwards, arrive at **Refuge les Grands (2113m)**.

This narrow section of path is cut into the cliffs

V1E

S See Map 1d. Descend SE from the refuge. After a few minutes, descend an exposed and exhilarating section of path cut into the cliffs which has been paved with stone: there is a cable to assist but watch your footing.

1 1:30: TR at a junction. Immediately afterwards, cross a bridge to arrive beside **Chalet du Glacier**. TL and continue on a beautiful balcony path heading down the valley.

2 1:50: Keep SH at a junction ('Col de la Forclaz'). At the next junction, keep SH.

F 2:00: Arrive at **Col de la Forclaz (1526m)**.

Time	2:00
Distance	6.0
Ascent	20
Descent	607
Maximum Altitude	2113
Refreshments on route	Chalet du Glacier (1:30) Col de la Forclaz
Accommodation	Col de la Forclaz

Refuge les Grands to Col de la Forclaz

V1E

Refuge les Grands overlooks the Glacier du Trient

This is the continuation of the variant route which was commenced on Stage v1d. The views of Glacier du Trient on the steep descent are stunning. Like Stage v1d, the route is quiet, with most people opting to stay on the main WHR.

The descent is long and steep. Just after leaving the refuge, take care on an exposed section of path cut into the cliffs and protected with a cable.

The hotel at Col de la Forclaz is the only place to stay and it can be very busy with groups: reserve in advance. If you cannot get a booking, then you could avoid Col de la Forclaz altogether by leaving Stage v1e at Chalet du Glacier and proceeding on Stage 2b directly to Arpette: this makes for an incredible but challenging day.

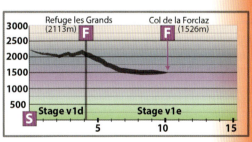

Col de la Forclaz can be seen from the incredible balcony path on Stage v1d

The view from Refuge du Peuty

Le Peuty to Col de la Forclaz

The hamlet of le Peuty

A short climb through forest to Col de la Forclaz. The popular hotel at the col is the only place to stay and it can be very busy with groups: reserve in advance. You can avoid Col de la Forclaz altogether by leaving Stage 2a at the junction mentioned at waypoint no. 2 below and then continuing directly on Stage 2b towards Fenêtre d'Arpette.

S See Map 1d. From Refuge du Peuty head E on a small road which becomes a track. Cross a road and climb N on a path.

1 0:20: At a junction, there are two paths heading towards the N: take the right-hand one.

2 0:30: Cross a modern footbridge over a road and climb steeply on a path. Soon, at a junction, TL to head to Col de la Forclaz: alternatively, TR to start Stage 2b, avoiding Col de la Forclaz.

F 0:45: Arrive at **Col de la Forclaz (1526m)**.

Time	0:45
Distance	2.1
Ascent	200
Descent	0
Maximum Altitude	1526
Refreshments on route	Col de la Forclaz
Accommodation	Col de la Forclaz

Relais d'Arpette has a fabulous rural location

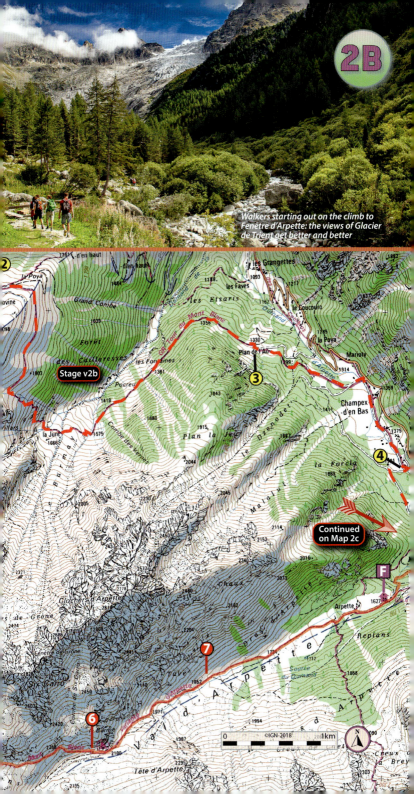

Walkers starting out on the climb to Fenêtre d'Arpette: the views of Glacier de Trient get better and better

The unforgettable path has grandstand views of the Glacier du Trient

Col de la Forclaz to Arpette

2B

The descent through Val d'Arpette is a relaxing contrast to the struggles near the col

The col known as Fenêtre d'Arpette (2665m) is a highlight of the WHR. Pray for a clear day as the view of the Glacier du Trient to the SW is exceptional: it is hard to describe just how close to it you get. One walker complained to us that after posting selfies of himself with the glacier on social media, he was bombarded with accusations of photo tampering! But the stage is not all about the col, for the scenery on both sides of it is amazing.

This is one of the hardest routes on the WHR and should not be underestimated. The final section of the climb, across rocks, is steep and unstable. The initial descent from the col is also steep and unstable so watch your footing. The subsequent section across boulders is very challenging: often there is no path and some scrambling is required. It would be easy to fall from the boulders, injuring yourself seriously, so take it slowly and choose your steps carefully.

The sections without any path make navigation more difficult. Sometimes snow can lie near the col until early July. In such conditions, it would be unwise to attempt this route: it would be treacherous and difficult to navigate. Also, avoid this stage in bad weather or low visibility when route finding would be tricky: in such conditions use the Stage v2b variant.

The Fenêtre d'Arpette is a small place and you are unlikely to have it to yourself as it is also popular with TMB trekkers: start early to beat the crowds. Relais d'Arpette is a beautiful place to stay but most people opt to continue to Champex.

Joubarbe

2B

Time	6:00
Distance	12.2
Ascent	1149
Descent	1048
Maximum Altitude	2665
Refreshments on route	Chalet du Glacier (0:40) Relais d'Arpette
Accommodation	Relais d'Arpette

S See Map 2b. Head S from the hotel, crossing a road to a yellow signpost. Keep SH ('Fenêtre d'Arpette') and continue on a path contouring around the hillside (the same path that is travelled at the end of Stage v1e). Soon, walk beside an old irrigation canal. Keep SH at any junctions for now.

1 0:40: TL at a junction to arrive at **Chalet du Glacier**: there is a tepee here that can be booked for the night. Just afterwards, bear left ('Arpette'). After 10min, TL at a junction ('Fenêtre d'Arpette'). As the path climbs, you get closer to the glacier.

2 1:35: Take care on a precipitous section of path protected by a rope: a fall would be serious. After a while, pass to the left of an old cabin.

3 2:35: Eventually, bear left and climb a rocky gully, following waymarks: watch your footing. Finally, scramble up a very steep section.

4 3:30: Cross the narrow **Fenêtre d'Arpette (2665m)**. On a fine day you will want to spend some time here. Descend steeply E on a path that soon splinters into a series of interlinking ones. Watch your footing as the surface is unstable.

5 3:45: In a rocky gully, follow waymarks and cairns across large boulders. This section is challenging as often there is no path. It would be easy to fall from the boulders so take it slowly and choose your steps carefully. After another steep descent, enter a huge mountain bowl: the path descends, more gently now, along the left flank of it.

6 4:50: TL at a junction.

7 5:30: TL at a junction ('Champex') and descend on a track.

F 6:00: Pass through a gate at some chalets and descend on a track. Soon afterwards, arrive at **Relais d'Arpette (1627m)**.

The descent towards Champex is steep and rocky in places but the views are exquisite

V2B

S See Map 2b. From the hotel, head E across the road and pick up a path to the left of the shop. Soon, start to climb through forest.

① 1:50: Cross a small col and start to descend.

② 2:00: Pass the idyllic farm buildings at **Bovine (1987m)** where there is a lovely buvette. Keep descending as the path contours around the hillside with magnificent views of the Rhône Valley. After a while, drop below the tree line and descend more steeply: watch out for loose rocks. Take care crossing a few streams particularly in early summer when there can be a lot of water.

③ 3:30: Pass the little buvette at **Plan de l'Au**. Shortly afterwards, TR onto a path. At a junction, keep SH on a track. Keep SH at another junction. Just afterwards, cross a bridge. Immediately afterwards, TR. Pass through **Champex-d'en-Bas**.

④ 4:00: Now see Map 2c. Soon TR at a junction, climbing: alternatively, keep SH if you wish to stay at Gîte Bon Abri. A few minutes later, TL onto a forest track. After 20min, TR onto a main road: take care at blind corners. Pass the campsite on the left.

F 4:45: Arrive at **Champex-Lac (1467m)**.

Col de la Forclaz to Champex (via Bovine)

V2B

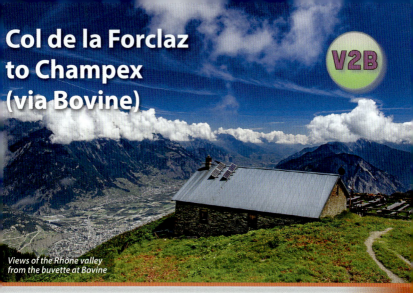

Views of the Rhône valley from the buvette at Bovine

Climb through aromatic forest with tantalising views of high peaks between the trees. Emerge from the forest at the stunning pastures around Bovine where there is a buvette: stop for a drink or some food, enjoying the sublime views of the Rhône Valley stretching out towards the E. Shortly afterwards, descend steeply as you head towards Champex. The slopes are covered with Alpenrose which is a vibrant pink colour in June/July.

Time	4:45
Distance	14.8
Ascent	741
Descent	790
Maximum Altitude	2049
Refreshments on route	Bovine (2:00) Plan de l'Au (3:30) Gîte Bon Abri (4:00) Champex
Accommodation	Gîte Bon Abri (4:00) Champex

This is a very underrated variant because the main WHR (Stage 2b) is so incredible. In fact, many people walk Stage v2b only because the weather is too bad to undertake Stage 2b. That is a shame because it is a very beautiful route in its own right. It is also a much easier option for those who have doubts about the boulder crossings on Stage 2b. The descent from Bovine is quite steep and there is some loose rock on the surface of the path.

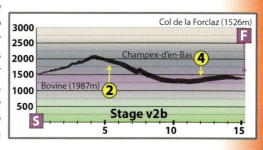

The magnificent lake at Champex

Arpette to Champex

2C

The beautiful fountain in the centre of Champex

A short, pretty stage involving a simple descent into the stunning lakeside town of Champex-Lac. As is often the case with place names in French, the correct pronunciation of Champex is not immediately obvious (even to French speakers). It is the subject of much discussion amongst walkers: some French speakers pronounce the 'x' and some do not. The directions for this stage are a little fiddly.

Time	0:45
Distance	2.4
Ascent	0
Descent	161
Maximum Altitude	1627
Refreshments on route	Champex
Accommodation	Champex

S Descend on the track. Shortly afterwards, TL on a path ('Champex'). After a few minutes, TL across a bridge. Just afterwards, TR on a path heading downhill alongside a torrent. Soon, cross the torrent again on a bridge.

1 0:15: Shortly afterwards, TL at a junction. After a while, TL on another path. Shortly afterwards, at a ski lift, TL. Keep SH under the cables of another ski lift. Just afterwards, TL onto a road ('Champex').

2 0:35: Shortly afterwards, when you arrive at the main road, turn sharp right and head S on a path. Follow the path around to the left, cross a bridge and then TL on another path. Shortly afterwards, keep SH ahead at a junction. TL at the next junction. Shortly afterwards, TR on a grassy path. Immediately afterwards, TL towards a boardwalk. Then TL on a tarmac lane.

F 0:45: Shortly afterwards, TR to walk along the main street of **Champex-Lac (1467m)**.

S Walk SE alongside the lake on a path. Just after the lake, TL on a road. Follow the road around to the left past Hôtel Splendide. Just after Hôtel Alpina, TR and descend on a path ('Sembrancher'): ignore offshoots. Keep SH across a gravel track to descend on a path.

1 0:50: TR at a fork (yellow sign). A few minutes later, TL at a junction ('Sembrancher').

2 1:10: TL on a track. Immediately afterwards, TR downhill on a path ('Sembrancher'). Keep SH onto a track which soon becomes a path. TL just before a trough at the hamlet of Soulalex ('Sembrancher'). Soon, TL onto another road. Shortly afterwards, TL at a fork ('Sembrancher'). At a fork beside a park bench, TR (yellow sign). After 15min, cross a track and descend on a path.

3 2:00: Walk through the village of **la Garde (900m)**, following the signs for 'Sembrancher'. Leave the village on a road. Keep SH across a junction. Soon the road bends to the left and becomes a track (yellow sign). Keep on this track, following yellow signs, until it turns sharply right at an electricity pylon: keep SH to pick up a grassy path (yellow waymarks). TR onto a gravel track ('Sembrancher'). Take care crossing a road and continue downhill on a path.

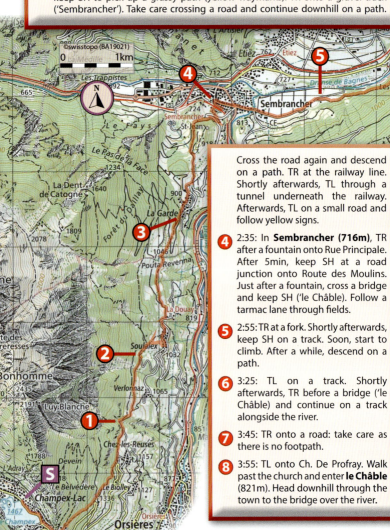

Cross the road again and descend on a path. TR at the railway line. Shortly afterwards, TL through a tunnel underneath the railway. Afterwards, TL on a small road and follow yellow signs.

4 2:35: In **Sembrancher (716m)**, TR after a fountain onto Rue Principale. After 5min, keep SH at a road junction onto Route des Moulins. Just after a fountain, cross a bridge and keep SH ('le Châble'). Follow a tarmac lane through fields.

5 2:55: TR at a fork. Shortly afterwards, keep SH on a track. Soon, start to climb. After a while, descend on a path.

6 3:25: TL on a track. Shortly afterwards, TR before a bridge ('le Châble') and continue on a track alongside the river.

7 3:45: TR onto a road: take care as there is no footpath.

8 3:55: TL onto Ch. De Profray. Walk past the church and enter **le Châble (821m)**. Head downhill through the town to the bridge over the river.

Champex to le Châble

The valley scenery that accompanies you all the way down to Sembrancher

On this transition stage, travel away from the MB Massif towards the Combin Massif. It is a valley walk which is far removed from the previous high mountain stages and those to come. This part of Switzerland is gentle and green: forests of larch and pine and the bucolic, flower filled, 'Sound of Music' pastures that one associates with Switzerland. And dotted around are the neat and tidy chalets found only in Switzerland. A long but easy descent to the town of Sembrancher is followed by a short, gentle climb to le Châble.

The directions for this stage are a little complicated but the route is quite well served with yellow waymarks and signposts. If you stay overnight in le Châble then you are entitled to a free Verbier lift pass for the following day: ask for it when you check-in if you wish to avoid the tough climb on Stage 4.

Time	4:00
Distance	14.1
Ascent	192
Descent	837
Maximum Altitude	1470
Refreshments on route	le Châble
Accommodation	le Châble

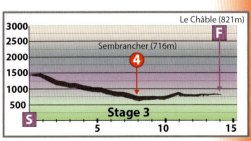

A relentless and long climb through the forests around the ski resort of Verbier keeps you occupied for much of the day. Fortunately, the excellent views help to take your mind off the exertion. Finally, the route rises above the trees and you are treated to the spectacular sight of the Grand Combin to the SE: this snowy peak will dominate proceedings for the next few days. You get to enjoy this view at length as the superb balcony path contours around the slopes all the way to Cabane du Mont Fort: a wonderful setting for an overnight stop. From there, the MB massif is also visible to the SW: sunrise can be spectacular.

Route finding on the entire climb requires careful attention: follow the directions closely and look out for yellow signs and waymarks. Start early to get well into the climb before the midday heat.

Most of the climb on this stage could be avoided by taking the cable car from le Châble to les Ruinettes which is no more than 10min from waypoint 9 (see map). If you stay overnight in le Châble then you are entitled to a free lift pass for the following day: ask for it when you check-in.

Stage 4 sees the first great views of Grand Combin

S Cross the bridge over the river and TL. TR onto Ch. des Etales. Just afterwards, TL at a junction and then follow signs for 'Forge Oreiller', and waymarks, up through the hamlet of Villette. TR just before the Forge.

1 0:15: Cross a road and climb Ch. du Reposoir. Soon, TR ('Chapelle des Verneys') onto Ch. du Four: do not go SH uphill following the sign for 'Mont Fort' (this leads to Verbier). After a few minutes, keep SH on a track. Shortly afterwards, TL on a path ('les Verneys').

2 0:35: In the hamlet of **Fontenelle**, at a junction beside a fountain, TR up Ch. du Grangeret. At the next junction, TR. Soon afterwards, TR onto a path. Climb steeply and after a few minutes, TR ('Chapelle des Verneys').

3 1:00: Continue past **Chapelle des Verneys**. After the buildings of the hamlet of **les Verneys**, descend gently. A few minutes later, TL on a path between trees ('Sarreyer').

4 1:40: TL at a junction ('Clambin') and climb steeply.

5 2:20: TL on a broad track. Shortly afterwards, TR at a fork. After a while, TR onto a path (yellow waymark): this junction is easy to miss. Follow yellow signs up through the trees. TL just after a farm building, contouring around the hillside. Take care as this narrow path runs along the edge of some steep drops.

6 3:00: TR at a junction ('Clambin') and climb. After a steep climb, the path levels and passes some chalets.

7 3:30: A few minutes later, arrive at a junction at **Clambin (1728m)** near a restaurant: TR ('le Hattey'). Verbier can be seen to the NW.

8 4:00: At Hatay, TR at a junction ('Mont Fort'). After a few minutes, follow the track around to the left. After 15min, TR on a path ('les Ruinettes') passing through myrtille and raspberry shrubs. Take care as the path crosses some mountain biking tracks. Around 2100 m, start to emerge from the trees with stunning consequences.

9 4:55: At a junction, TR on a track: again, watch out for mountain bikes. After a few minutes, the track becomes a path heading steeply uphill. Shortly afterwards, TR, taking the middle of three paths ('Mont Fort') and contour around the hillside. A few minutes later, TL on another path ('Mont Fort'). Shortly, cross a track and continue uphill on a path ('Mont Fort') which makes a magnificent traverse around the hillside. Eventually, you should spot Cabane du Mont Fort up ahead on a rock outcrop to the E.

10 5:50: Cross a track and continue SH on a path ('Mont Fort'). Soon TR onto a path (yellow waymarks). Pass underneath the cabane and then TL at a junction ('Mont Fort').

F 6:15: 10min later, arrive at **Cabane du Mont Fort (2456m)**.

Time	6:15
Distance	12.3
Ascent	1665
Descent	30
Maximum Altitude	2456
Refreshments on route	Clambin (3:30) Cabane du Mont Fort
Accommodation	Cabane du Mont Fort

4

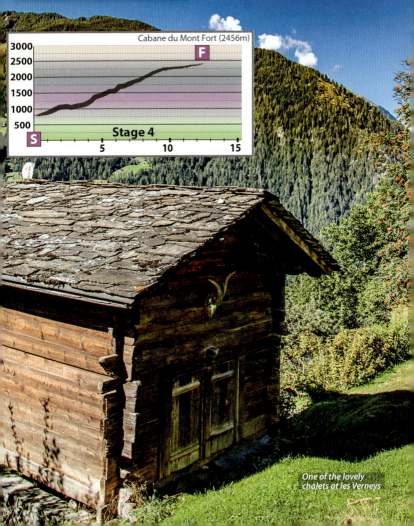

One of the lovely chalets at les Verneys

Cabane de Prafleuri

Time	6:30
Distance	13.9
Ascent	960
Descent	754
Maximum Altitude	2987
Refreshments on route	Cabane de Prafleuri
Accommodation	Cabane de Prafleuri

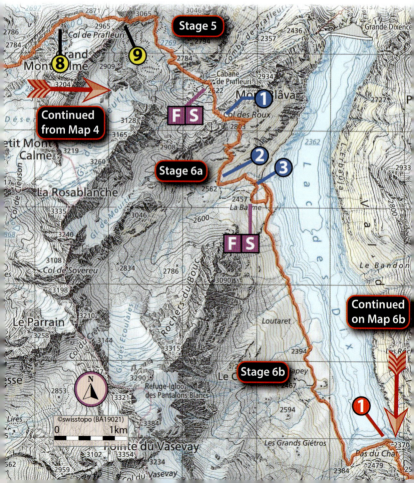

Cabane du Mont Fort to Cabane de Prafleuri

The Mont Blanc massif seen from near Col Termin

For those who like their mountain walks to be wild, this stage will be a highlight of the WHR: much of the route is remote with few signs of human habitation. And you will cross three wonderful, and very different, cols.

After leaving the cabane, climb to Col Termin, enjoying the WHR's last great views of the MB Massif: you are in for a treat if you walk this section as the sun is rising. There are plenty of Ibex and Chamois so keep your eyes peeled.

The highlight of the stage is the next section between Col Termin and Col de Louvie: initially, a remote, beautiful landscape of grassy slopes and snowy peaks which overlooks the shimmering blue Lac de Louvie. The views of Grand Combin are exquisite too. Soon, the grass gives way to rock as you climb towards Col de Louvie where both Grand Combin and Mont Blanc are visible.

After Col de Louvie, enter a remote moonscape of barren moraine: the boulders and glacial lakes are a stark contrast to what has come before. It would be easy to lose your way here so take care with navigation. Eventually, climb steeply to the third and final pass, Col de Prafleuri. Then descend steeply to Cabane de Prafleuri, set on an outcrop overlooking a barren cirque and surrounded by peaks.

This stage is a tough one as the terrain is often rocky and uneven. It undulates regularly and there are many sections of rocks and boulders: watch your footing and follow waymarks. Also take care on some narrow, precipitous sections, a few of which are protected with chains fixed to the rock.

The whole stage is well waymarked: blue/white shortly after leaving the cabane; red/white for the rest of the stage. However, in bad weather, low visibility or if there was some snow still lying, navigation would be challenging. In particular, navigation after Col de Louvie requires careful attention.

The landscape of rock and tarns is best viewed from Col de Prafleuri

S See Map 4. Take the path heading E from the rear of the cabane ('Col Termin') and descend. TR at a junction. Immediately afterwards, TL at a blue signpost (blue/white waymarks) onto a narrow path. After a few minutes, TR and descend on a track. Shortly afterwards, leave the track for a path (blue signpost). Take care crossing a few streams. Soon, traverse SW across the face of the slope, heading directly towards the MB Massif. After a while, the faint, narrow path starts to climb more steeply: take care as the drops are steep.

1 1:20: Keep SH at a junction ('Col Termin'). A few minutes later, cross a rocky gully (cairns): do not stop here. Afterwards, take care on a precipitous section protected by chains.

2 2:00: Cross **Col Termin (2648m)** and descend on a path which quickly bears left to head NE. Almost immediately, Lac de Louvie appears to the SE. Soon, there are some narrow sections with precipitous drops.

3 2:20: Keep SH at a junction ('Col de Louvie'): climb and then cross a boulder field. Afterwards, the undulating path contours around the hillside.

4 2:50: Enter a huge boulder field: watch your footing and follow waymarks. Soon, the path undulates again.

5 3:15: Keep SH at a junction ('Col de Louvie'): the path to the left comes from Col de la Chaux (Stage v5).

6 3:40: Cross **Col de Louvie (2921m)**. Head initially E through a barren, rocky landscape (waymarks). Shortly, start to descend steeply: the path is faint and hard to follow. Soon the glacier, Grand Désert appears to the right.

7 4:05: Pass along the left side of a lake: at a huge boulder on the N side of it, TR and head SE (waymarks/cairns). Cross the outflow stream of the lake and head E on a faint path. After 20min, bear left at a signpost beside a large boulder and head NE ('Col de Prafleuri'). After climbing, the gradient levels: proceed across a rocky plateau.

8 4:50: See Map 5. Descend towards three turquoise lakes: the path is steep and rocky. There are a few short sections where scrambling is required. Soon, the faint path heads to the left of the lakes. After the lakes, climb steeply through a boulder field. When the path disappears, scramble over boulders (waymarks).

9 5:30: TL at **Col de Prafleuri (2987m)** ('Prafleuri') and soon descend steeply. After 20min, cross a barren plateau. Then, descend through hillocks. TR at a junction onto a track. After a few minutes, TL on a path.

F 6:30: Finally, climb for a few minutes to arrive at **Cabane de Prafleuri (2662m)**.

The views of Grand Combin on Stage 5 are a highlight of the WHR

The barren landscape between Col de Louvie and Col de Prafleuri

S See Map 4. Take the path heading NE from the rear of the cabane. Keep NE at a junction, continuing on a track. At the next junction, turn sharp left. Soon the track bends right to head SE.

1 0:45: TR onto a path (2704m). Follow cairns and waymarks through rocky terrain: sometimes the path disappears.

2 1:45: Cross **Col de la Chaux (2939m)** and head into a rocky cirque.

3 2:10: TL at a junction and soon pass to the right of **Lac du Petit Mont Fort (2763m)**.

4 2:30: TL at a junction where you meet Stage 5 at waypoint 5. Follow the Stage 5 directions to Cabane de Prafleuri.

F 5:45: See Map 5. Arrive at **Cabane de Prafleuri (2662m)**.

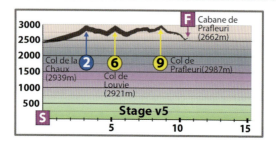

Cabane du Mont Fort to Cabane de Prafleuri (via Col de la Chaux)

The incredible path to Col de Louvie

This variant shortens Stage 5 by avoiding the detour to Col Termin and taking a more direct route straight over Col de la Chaux. Some suggest that this is a bad weather alternative but we disagree: Col de la Chaux is no place to get caught in low visibility. And, in any case, Stage v5 still requires you to travel between Col de Louvie and Col de Prafleuri, a barren place where navigation is tricky. Although, the route over Col de la Chaux is a fine walk in its own right, we still prefer Stage 5. It is, however, useful if you are short of time.

The terrain is often rocky and uneven. There are sections of rocks and boulders: watch your footing and follow waymarks. Also, take care on some narrow, precipitous sections. In bad weather, low visibility or if there was some snow still lying, navigation would be challenging. In particular, navigation after Col de Louvie requires careful attention.

Ibex are commonly seen near Cabane du Mont Fort

Time	5:45
Distance	10.6
Ascent	987
Descent	781
Maximum Altitude	2987
Refreshments on route	Cabane de Prafleuri
Accommodation	Cabane de Prafleuri

The view from Refuge de la Gentiane, la Barmaz

S See Map 5. From a signpost in front of the cabane, follow a path heading SE ('Col des Roux'). Follow cairns through a stony plateau and pick up the path on the other side.

1 0:30: Bear left at **Col des Roux (2804m)** and traverse the hillside on a path ('la Barma'). Soon the path starts to descend gently. After 10-15min, cross a short section of boulders following waymarks.

2 1:10: Pass the unmanned **Cabane les Ecoulaies (2575m)**. There are blankets and a wood-burning cooker but you would have to bring your own food to stay there. The setting is lovely but it is not as well-kept as Refuge de la Gentiane.

3 1:25: TR at a junction ('Refuge la Barma'). Shortly afterwards, cross a bridge.

F 1:30: 5min later, arrive at **Refuge de la Gentiane (2457m)** at la Barmaz.

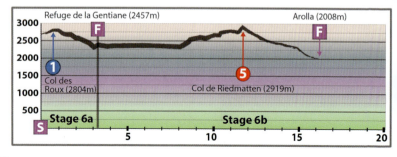

Cabane de Prafleuri to Refuge de la Gentiane

6A

The exquisite path above the other-worldly Lac des Dix

A short climb out of the barren terrain surrounding Cabane de Prafleuri leads to Col des Roux where you are met by an entirely new, and starkly contrasting, vista: grassy slopes, snowy peaks, glaciers and the incredible Lac des Dix. The colour of the lake is other-worldly and the descent to Refuge de la Gentiane is Alpine walking at its finest. The normally unmanned refuge makes for one of the best overnight stops on the WHR. It is spotlessly clean and fully equipped with blankets and a wood-fired cooker: you will need to bring your own food unless you are lucky enough to arrive at a weekend when the hut is manned.

Refuge de la Gentiane

Time	1:30
Distance	3.2
Ascent	194
Descent	399
Maximum Altitude	2804
Refreshments on route	Refuge de la Gentiane
Accommodation	Refuge de la Gentiane

The famous Pigne d'Arolla (3796m)

S See Map 5. Facing the lake, TR onto the path in front of the refuge. At a track near the shore of the lake, TR and walk S alongside the lake. At the SW tip of the lake, cross a bridge, bear left and continue following the track along the lake's S side.

1 1:15: TR and climb on a steep path ('Col de Riedmatten'). After 10min, keep SH, heading S amongst rocky crags: ignore a path on the left and instead follow a sign for 'Dix' painted on a rock. Also ignore a confusing sign for 'Col de Riedmatten' painted on another rock.

2 1:55: See Map 6b. Arrive at a fork: TR for Stage v6b to Cabane des Dix. Otherwise TL to continue on Stage 6b ('Col de Riedmatten') and descend into a rocky moraine. Cross a bridge. Immediately afterwards, TR and climb the valley on a path.

3 2:15: Head N and then E around a plateau. After 5min, head NE up a rocky slope. Soon, the path bends right to the SE, sometimes disappearing over rocks. After a while, descend steeply through boulders: the path is unstable and difficult to follow.

4 2:55: The path bears left, heading E straight up an extremely steep and unstable slope. Take great care and do not attempt this section in bad weather or after rain. You will need to use your hands. After 10min, arrive at a faint junction which has directions painted on rocks. TL for Col de Riedmatten or TR for the alternative route over Pas de Chèvres (see box). From the junction, the path to Col de Riedmatten is clearer and can be walked rather than scrambled but it is still steep and unstable. The final approach to the col has chains to assist.

5 3:20: Cross **Col de Riedmatten (2919m)** and descend on a clear path ('Arolla').

6 3:40: TL at a junction ('Arolla'): the path descending from the right is the alternative route arriving from Pas de Chèvres.

7 4:15: Cross a bridge and continue downhill to the E. After about 25min, keep SH at a junction on a path ('Arolla'). TL after a chalet ('Arolla'). Shortly afterwards, descend on a track. After a few minutes, TR on a path (yellow sign). Soon, TL at a faint junction: from here, there is a confusing array of paths so keep following the waymarks.

8 5:20: TR and keep downhill on a track past Grand Hôtel Kurhaus. Shortly afterwards, TR on a track ('Arolla').

F 5:30: Arrive in **Arolla (2008m)**.

Time	5:30
Distance	13.0
Ascent	641
Descent	1090
Maximum Altitude	2919
Refreshments on route	Arolla
Accommodation	Arolla

Refuge de la Gentiane to Arolla

6B

It could be you! The incredible descent towards Arolla

An easy stroll beside the spectacular Lac des Dix leads to probably the most challenging section of the WHR. At the SE tip of the lake, head up into a barren but spectacular glacial valley dominated by the peak of Mont Blanc de Cheilon (3870m). Then, climb very steeply up the E flank of the valley to Col de Riedmatten, a narrow cleft between rocks: the views are excellent. A long descent follows all the way to the lovely village of Arolla which is a popular base for mountaineers.

The climb amongst boulders before the col is extremely steep, rocky and unstable. Rockfalls and landslides frequently damage the path and some scrambling is required: take great care on this section and do not attempt it in bad weather or low visibility. After rain, landslides could occur which would be dangerous.

Between the lake and the col, navigation is tricky: often the path disappears over rocks. Fortunately, the waymarking is much improved these days: red/white waymarks. Look out for Chamois in this area.

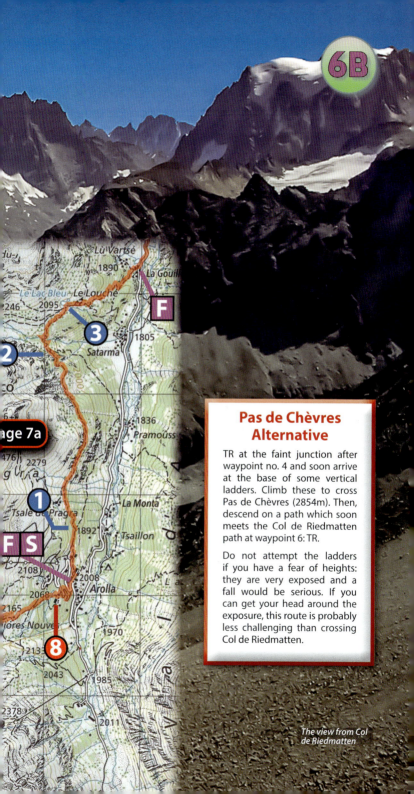

6B

Pas de Chèvres Alternative

TR at the faint junction after waypoint no. 4 and soon arrive at the base of some vertical ladders. Climb these to cross Pas de Chèvres (2854m). Then, descend on a path which soon meets the Col de Riedmatten path at waypoint 6: TR.

Do not attempt the ladders if you have a fear of heights: they are very exposed and a fall would be serious. If you can get your head around the exposure, this route is probably less challenging than crossing Col de Riedmatten.

The view from Col de Riedmatten

Mont Blanc de Cheilon seen from Col de Riedmatten

Refuge de la Gentiane to Arolla (via Cabane des Dix)

V6B

Cabane des Dix has a commanding position, overlooking Mont Blanc de Cheilon and the Glacier de Cheilon

This fantastic variant enables you to stay at Cabane des Dix, magnificently situated next to Mont Blanc de Cheilon and the Glacier de Cheilon: a night here is not easily forgotten. Like Stage 6b, this stage heads across probably the most challenging section of the WHR. The route is shared with Stage 6b all the way up into the barren glacial valley. But then, instead of following Stage 6b up the valley floor, head up a fabulous ridge all the way to the cabane. Then, after a tough moraine crossing, meet up with Stage 6b again.

Both Col de Riedmatten and Pas de Chèvres are serious undertakings so read the Stage 6b warnings which apply equally to Stage v6b. Stage v6b is a little longer and harder than Stage 6b.

Time	6:30
Distance	16.0
Ascent	846
Descent	1295
Maximum Altitude	2928
Refreshments on route	Cabane des Dix (3:00) Arolla
Accommodation	Cabane des Dix (3:00) Arolla

S See Map 6b. Follow Stage 6b to the fork at waypoint 2: TR, heading generally S up a ridge.

3 3:00: Arrive at **Cabane des Dix (2928m)**. Head S on a path which soon bends SE and then NE across moraine (waymarks, cairns and markers).

4 3:55: Arrive at waypoint 4 of Stage 6b. Now follow the Stage 6b directions again.

F 6:30: Arrive in **Arolla (2008m)**.

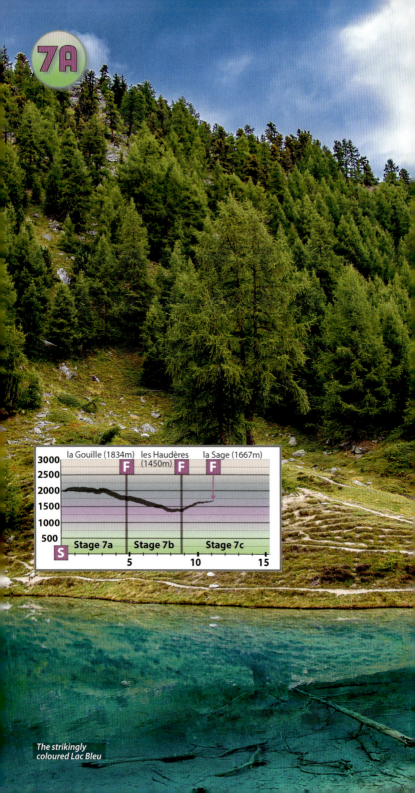

The strikingly coloured Lac Bleu

Arolla to la Gouille

7A

The exposed path to Lac Bleu

A short and underrated section of the WHR which is more tiring than it looks on paper: the climb to the stunning Lac Bleu, with its clear blue waters, is undulating so it involves more height gain than the start/finish altitudes would suggest. After the lake, pass le Louché, a lovely hamlet which has a little buvette where you can buy local cheese. Finish at the hotel/restaurant at la Gouille. The views throughout the stage are consistently excellent. Before Lac Bleu, take care on some exposed sections protected with cables.

Stages 7a, 7b and 7c together make for a relatively short day so the hotel at la Gouille is quite useful: you could tag Stage 7a onto Stage 6b, overnight at la Gouille and then complete Stages 7b, 7c and 8 the following day.

S See Map 6b. From the tourist office, head NE down a road. Shortly afterwards, TL climbing on a path ('Lac Bleu'). Soon, pass to the right of a building. Shortly afterwards, keep SH on a path heading N: ignore offshoots.

1 0:15: TL at a junction ('Lac Bleu'). The path undulates and there are frequent gains and losses of altitude. Take care on exposed sections protected with cables.

2 1:00: Keep SH at a junction ('Lac Bleu').

3 1:30: Cross the bridge to the right of **Lac Bleu (2091m)** and TR, descending on a path. Shortly afterwards, TR at the beautiful hamlet of le Louché (2079m) ('la Gouille'). Afterwards, continue descending, ignoring offshoots.

F 2:00: Arrive at the hotel at **la Gouille (1834m)**.

Time	2:00
Distance	4.8
Ascent	252
Descent	426
Maximum Altitude	2141
Refreshments on route	Le Louché (1:35) La Gouille
Accommodation	La Gouille

The descent into Arolla (Stage 6b)

La Gouille to les Haudères

7B

The long scenic descent to les Haudères

A short, scenic valley walk, descending all the way to the historical village of les Haudères with its immaculately preserved Valaisian barns and houses: notice how they are perched on stilts topped with large stone slabs to prevent rodents from entering.

S Cross the main road and TL to walk on a path alongside it. After a few minutes, TR on a path. At any junctions, follow yellow/black waymarks.

1 1:00: Approaching the hamlet of **Pralovin**, TL on a lane. A few minutes later, TR on a road. Then, cross a bridge and immediately afterwards, TL on a track. When you meet the road again, keep SH.

2 1:10. Cross the bridge at the entrance of les Haudères. TR onto Route de la Sage. After a few minutes, TL on Route du Vieux Village.

F 1:15: Walk through the old village of **les Haudères (1450m)** amongst the most incredible old barns and houses.

Time	1:15
Distance	4.0
Ascent	20
Descent	404
Maximum Altitude	1834
Refreshments on route	Les Haudères
Accommodation	Les Haudères

One of the magnificent chalets in the hamlet of la Sage

7C

Les Haudères to la Sage

The rural hamlet of la Sage is a lovely place to spend the night

Another short stage which climbs to the hamlet of la Sage, a lovely place to relax for the night before the exertions of Stage 8. There is only a hotel and a gîte so it is wise to book ahead.

S Map 7b. At a fork in the village, head N ('la Sage'). Keep SH, climbing on a tiled track which soon becomes a grassy one.

1 0:15: At a right-hand hairpin, keep SH on a path. 5min later, TR at a fork (no waymarks).

2 0:30: Keep SH up a road. Shortly afterwards, TL on another road ('la Sage').

F 0:45: Follow the road all the way up to the village of **la Sage (1667m)**.

Time	0:45
Distance	2.3
Ascent	230
Descent	13
Maximum Altitude	1667
Refreshments on route	La Sage
Accommodation	La Sage

103

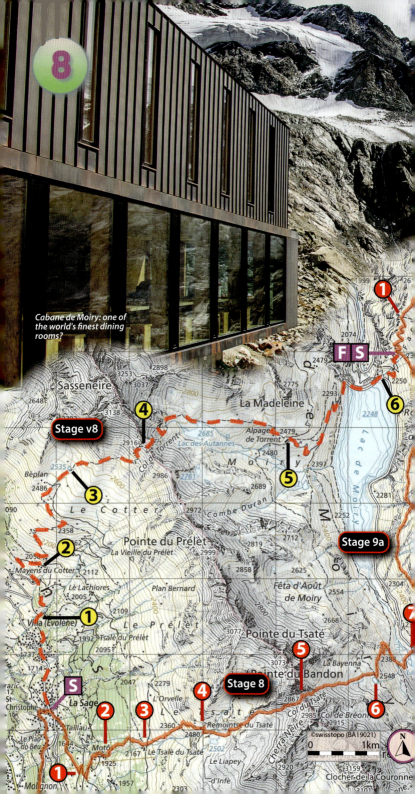

Cabane de Moiry: one of the world's finest dining rooms?

La Sage to Cabane de Moiry

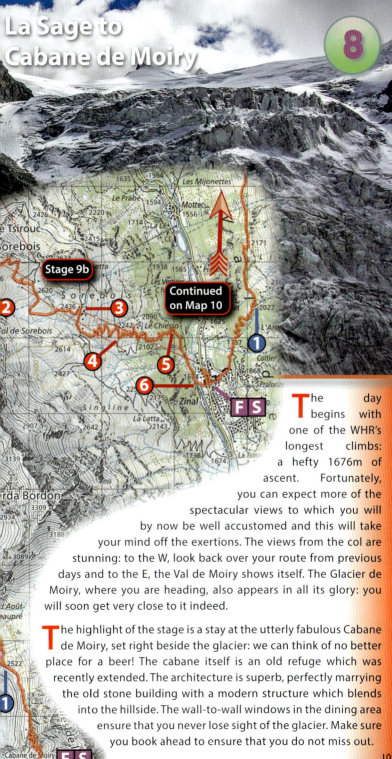

The day begins with one of the WHR's longest climbs: a hefty 1676m of ascent. Fortunately, you can expect more of the spectacular views to which you will by now be well accustomed and this will take your mind off the exertions. The views from the col are stunning: to the W, look back over your route from previous days and to the E, the Val de Moiry shows itself. The Glacier de Moiry, where you are heading, also appears in all its glory: you will soon get very close to it indeed.

The highlight of the stage is a stay at the utterly fabulous Cabane de Moiry, set right beside the glacier: we can think of no better place for a beer! The cabane itself is an old refuge which was recently extended. The architecture is superb, perfectly marrying the old stone building with a modern structure which blends into the hillside. The wall-to-wall windows in the dining area ensure that you never lose sight of the glacier. Make sure you book ahead to ensure that you do not miss out.

105

A stay in Cabane de Moiry is a highlight of the WHR

Time	5:45
Distance	10.9
Ascent	1676
Descent	518
Maximum Altitude	2867
Refreshments on route	Cabane de Moiry
Accommodation	Cabane de Moiry

The route is generally well waymarked with either yellow or red/white markings. The final climb to Cabane de Moiry is steep, rocky and exposed: there are a few sections where you will need to use your hands and there are some fixed cables. Look out for Ibex and Chamois on the climb to the cabane.

If you stay overnight at Cabane de Moiry then you are entitled to a free Zinal lift pass for the following day: ask for it when you check-in. You could use it to descend by cable car from Sorebois to Zinal, avoiding much of the descent on Stage 9b.

S From the road junction near Gîte l'Ecureuil, descend on a road ('Col du Tsaté'). Shortly afterwards, TL on a lane and climb. Soon, keep SH on a track through forest.

1 0:20: TL at a junction ('Col du Tsaté'). A few minutes later, TR (yellow sign). After 10min, at another junction, take the left of two paths (yellow signs). Shortly afterwards, TR on another path (yellow waymarks).

2 0:45: The path passes to the left of the buildings of the spectacular hamlet of **Motô (1925m)**. Keep SH at a junction.

3 1:15: Pass the hamlet of **le Tsaté (2167m)**. Afterwards, cross a track and climb steeply to the NE on a path ('Col du Tsaté') which heads through beautiful pastures filled with wildflowers. After 25min, keep SH across a track and continue on a path.

4 2:00: After the farm buildings at **Remointse du Tsaté (2480m)**, TR on a track. Shortly afterwards, TL on a path ('Col du Tsaté'): the path splinters and is tricky to follow. Soon, cross a grassy bowl with a lake beside it. Afterwards, climb NE.

5 3:15: Cross **Col du Tsaté (2867m)** and descend on a path ('Lac Bayenna') which is steep and unstable.

6 3:40: Pass to the left of **Lac de la Bayenna (2548m)**. Then, bear right briefly along the E side of it. Just afterwards, TL on a faint path heading N: this junction is not waymarked. After 20min, keep SH at a junction. Soon the path becomes rough and faint. After 5min, TL at a junction and follow a rough path.

7 4:10: TR at a car park (2352m) and climb E on a path ('Cabane de Moiry'). After a while, the path makes its way along the top of a little ridge: the views are incredible. Then, the path bears left dropping off the little ridge. Afterwards, climb on a path contouring upwards across the hillside. Soon, the gradient increases as the path climbs amongst rocks.

F 5:45: Finally, cross some boulders to arrive at **Cabane de Moiry (2825m)**.

The incredible vista to the SW from Col de Torrent

S See Map 8. From the road junction near Gîte l'Ecureuil, climb N on the road. At the chapel in Villa (Evolène), TR ('Col de Torrent'). Shortly afterwards, TR at a junction. Keep SH on a track: ignore offshoots.

1 0:40: Keep SH at a fork. Shortly, keep SH onto a path which soon crosses a stream. Climb N until you arrive at a farm road: then TR.

2 1:15: At **Mayens du Cotter (2058m)**, turn sharp left onto a path. Shortly afterwards, TR at a junction.

3 2:25: Pass a little tarn (2535m) and keep climbing.

4 3:45: Cross **Col de Torrent (2915m)** and descend NE. After 20min, pass the magnificent **Lac des Autannes (2685m)**.

5 4:30: At **Alpage de Torrent (2479m)**, head towards the SE on a track: follow it all the way to the dam at the N side of **Lac de Moiry (2250m)**. TR and walk across the top of the dam.

6 5:00: Arrive at the restaurant at the E side of the dam. Head initially E on a path and climb. After a few minutes, TL on a track. Shortly afterwards, TL on a path if you wish to stay at Gîte de Moiry: it is 5min away, just N of the dam. Otherwise, keep climbing on the track: you can cut across some of the hairpins.

F 5:15: Arrive at the **junction (2373m)** where Stage 9b begins.

La Sage to Barrage de Moiry (via Col de Torrent)

V8

Glacier de Moiry comes into view on the descent from Col de Torrent

Time	5:15
Distance	13.5
Ascent	1378
Descent	672
Maximum Altitude	2915
Refreshments on route	Barrage de Moiry
Accommodation	Barrage de Moiry

A spectacular alternative to Stage 8. The good news is that the vista from Col de Torrent is arguably superior to that at Col du Tsaté: the startlingly turquoise Lac de Moiry is just below to the E. The bad news is that you miss out on a night at Cabane de Moiry and therefore this variant is used mainly by those who are short of time.

The climb, up through pasture, is another big one but the views are excellent. However, the highlight is the sublime descent to Barrage de Moiry which is one of our favourite sections of the entire WHR. The accommodation at the end of the stage is the remote and peaceful Gîte de Moiry, just above the dam: you will have to descend briefly back to the restaurant at the dam for your evening meal.

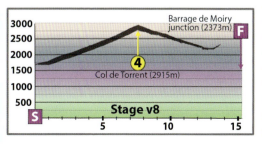

109

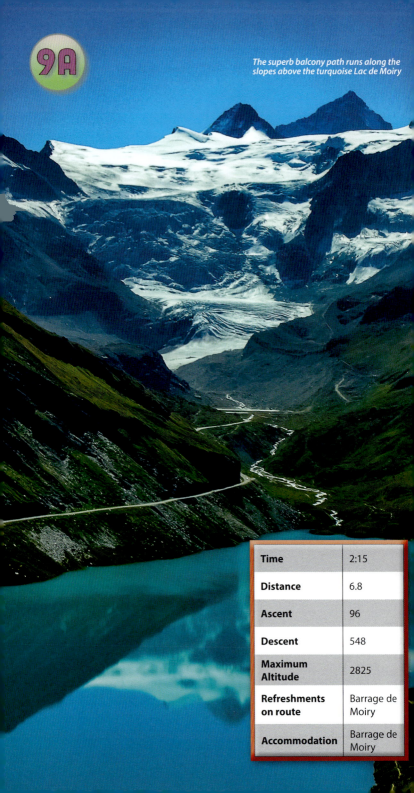

9A

The superb balcony path runs along the slopes above the turquoise Lac de Moiry

Time	2:15
Distance	6.8
Ascent	96
Descent	548
Maximum Altitude	2825
Refreshments on route	Barrage de Moiry
Accommodation	Barrage de Moiry

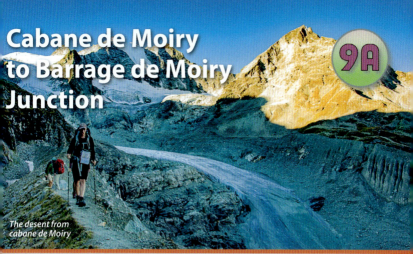

Cabane de Moiry to Barrage de Moiry Junction

9A

The desent from cabane de Moiry

Although you descend from Cabane de Moiry using the same path travelled on the previous stage, this is no imposition: you get to enjoy a different perspective of the Glacier de Moiry as it basks in the low light of sunrise. Anyway, you will soon leave this path, heading N on a superb balcony, high above the unforgettable, turquoise coloured, Lac de Moiry. On a fine day this is a highlight of the WHR.

Watch your footing on the descent from Cabane de Moiry as the path is steep and unstable. Look out for Ibex and Chamois on that section. The balcony path is undulating so it is more tiring than it looks on paper. Keep your eyes peeled for clumps of the rare Edelweiss.

> **S** See Map 8. Retrace your steps from the cabane and descend steeply.
>
> **1** 0:50: TR at a junction ('Moiry Barrage') onto a lovely path traversing the hillside. After 20min, keep SH at a junction ('Moiry Barrage'). Soon, get your first glimpse of Lac de Moiry. The path undulates with some quite big height gains and losses. Take care crossing some rocky stream beds and gullies, which can be quite slippery.
>
> **F** 2:15: Arrive at a **junction (2373m)**, above the Barrage de Moiry. This is where Stage v8 rejoins the main WHR. Descend on the track if you wish to stay at Gîte de Moiry: it is just below, about 50m above the dam.

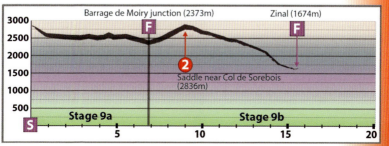

9B

Time	3:30
Distance	8.9
Ascent	478
Descent	1177
Maximum Altitude	2836
Refreshments on route	Sorebois (2:00) Zinal
Accommodation	Zinal

The magnificent path to Zinal

Barrage de Moiry Junction to Zinal

9B

Walkers climbing towards Col de Sorebois

Start with a steep climb to a saddle near Col de Sorebois: there are more fantastic views of Lac de Moiry all the way up. At the saddle, you are greeted by another incredible vista which is dominated by the Weisshorn (4506m) to the SE. Descend steeply through ski infrastructure to the small ski station of Sorebois with its lovely restaurant. Afterwards, leave the ski fields behind as you descend very steeply through beautiful pastures and forest to Zinal on the valley floor.

The descent from the saddle to Zinal is a 'knee-jerker'. You could avoid much of it by descending in the cable car from Sorebois to Zinal. If you stay overnight at Cabane de Moiry (Stage 8) then you are entitled to a free Zinal lift pass for the following day: ask for it when you check-in. For a timetable, see www.rma.ch.

S See Map 8. From the junction, climb on the grassy track ('Zinal').

1 0:20: TL on a path heading up to the NE: this junction is easy to miss (rock with a faint waymark).

2 1:30: Arrive at a **saddle (2836m)** just below the Corne de Sorebois (2895m): this saddle is slightly N of Col de Sorebois (as indicated on the map). TL if you wish to climb a few more metres to the summit of Corne de Sorebois. Otherwise, head NE across the saddle and pick up a path. Soon, TR onto a track and follow it downhill, ignoring offshoots. Eventually, the track bears right into a hanging valley, amongst ski infrastructure: keep on the track down through the valley.

3 2:00: TR at the ski station of **Sorebois (2436m)** ('Zinal'). There is a restaurant with a terrace overlooking the Weisshorn: a good place for a break. 5min later, TL on a path. Note that just afterwards there is an alternative track on the left which also goes to Zinal: it is less steep but longer.

4 2:35: TL onto a path (yellow sign). 10min later, TR at a junction ('Zinal'). Eventually, the path heads into trees and becomes very steep: take care.

5 3:10: TR at a junction ('Zinal'). After 5-10min, keep SH at a junction.

6 3:25: TL and cross a bridge. Shortly afterwards, keep SH up a small road and enter **Zinal (1675m)**.

Zinal to Gruben 10

The Matterhorn takes an unfamiliar wedge shape when viewed from above Zinal

Another incredible day out! A long ascent out of the Val d'Anniviers to Col de la Forcletta is followed by a long descent into the Turtmanntal Valley. On the climb, the Matterhorn shows itself but it appears wedge-shaped from this angle: very different to the familiar crooked form that it takes when viewed from Zermatt. The views from the col are exceptional (as usual). The ridge on which the col is situated is the dividing line between the French and German speaking parts of the Valais (or Wallis in German). The Turtmanntal is one of the most remote valleys in Switzerland and is completely cut off by winter snow.

Hotel Schwarzhorn (which has dormitories) is the only place to stay in Gruben itself and it is a good idea to book ahead, especially at weekends. Alternatively, there are beds at Pension-restaurant Waldesruh which is 5-10min further down the road from Gruben.

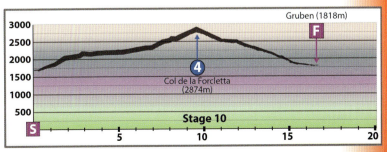

115

Time	6:15
Distance	16.8
Ascent	1270
Descent	1126
Maximum Altitude	2874
Refreshments on route	Gruben
Accommodation	Gruben

Adventurous goats in the pastures above Zinal

S See Map 8. From the tourist office, head briefly N down the road. Then TR on another road ('Hôtel Weisshorn'). Shortly afterwards, keep SH at a junction, ignoring yellow signs. TL before Hôtel Le Besso. Soon, TL on a track. Then keep SH across a road ('Hôtel Weisshorn').

1 0:40: TL at a junction and climb ('Hôtel Weisshorn'). After a while, the gradient eases and the path undulates. After 20min, climb a steep ramp to a junction: keep SH ('Hôtel Weisshorn'). Afterwards, the gradient eases again and you proceed on a superb balcony high above the valley.

2 1:40: See Map 10. Pass farm buildings at **Barneuza Alpage (2210m)**. Immediately afterwards, keep SH on a path ('Hôtel Weisshorn'), ignoring the path descending to the left. After 5min, cross boulders following waymarks.

3 2:15: TR at a junction (2340m), climbing on a path which is faint in places (waymarks). After 20min, pass the wooden cross at **Tsahèlett (2524m)**. The path now heads E across pastures and then zig-zags up a rocky slope.

4 4:00: Cross **Col de la Forcletta (2874m)**. Head NE down a shale slope into a rocky valley. Keep following a path down the valley beside a stream. After a while, the path bears left, leaving the stream.

5 4:45: Pass between the buildings of **Chalte Berg (2495m)**. Then head E on a path down a grassy slope (waymarks). TL onto a track. Shortly afterwards, bear right on a path running parallel to the road. At **Massstafel (2239m)**, TR onto a track. Just after a right-hand hairpin, TL on a path which soon enters forest. Zig-zag down to the E.

6 5:55: Pass to the left of some farm buildings and head N on a path to the left of the Turtmänna River

F 6:15: Cross the river on a bridge. Immediately afterwards, TL and enter **Gruben (1818m)**.

Hôtel Weisshorn is perched on the edge of the slopes with a wonderful outlook

After gaining height, there are grandstand views all the way to Hôtel Weisshorn

Time	3:45
Distance	11.3
Ascent	819
Descent	156
Maximum Altitude	2423
Refreshments on route	Hôtel Weisshorn
Accommodation	Hôtel Weisshorn

S See Map 8. Follow the Stage 10 directions to waypoint 3.

3 2:15: See Map 10. Keep SH at the junction (2340m). After 20min, keep SH at another junction.

4 2:55: TL on a track. Just afterwards, TR on a path. 5min later, descend briefly on a track. Shortly afterwards, TR on a path.

5 3:35: Just after a strange sculpture called 'Haley's Comet', TL at a fork (no waymark) and descend towards the hotel which can be seen ahead.

F 3:45: Finally, a short climb brings you to **Hôtel Weisshorn (2337m)**.

Zinal to Hôtel Weisshorn

V10A

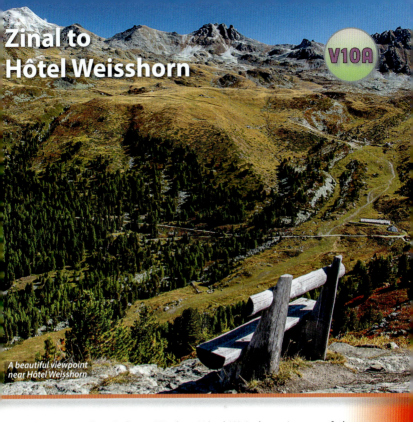

A beautiful viewpoint near Hôtel Weisshorn

The section of path from Zinal to Hôtel Weisshorn is one of the most stunning on the WHR. After a climb out of Zinal (on the same path as that used on Stage 10), continue on an amazing balcony path all the way to Hôtel Weisshorn. Looking backwards, there are great views of the Matterhorn: from this angle it is wedge shaped. The hillsides are carpeted with Myrtille and Alpenrose (which is a vibrant pink in early summer).

Hôtel Weisshorn was first opened in 1883 but was destroyed in a fire in 1889. It was re-opened in its current form in 1891. The materials for its construction were carried up by mule. Apparently, the piano was carried on the backs of six men! It is a fabulous place to spend the night.

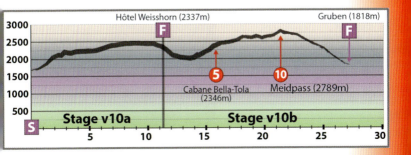

V10B

Time	5:30
Distance	16.0
Ascent	715
Descent	1234
Maximum Altitude	2789
Refreshments on route	Cabane Bella-Tola (1:25) Gruben
Accommodation	Cabane Bella-Tola (1:25) Gruben

Lac de l'Armina is set in a remote cirque, surrounded by rocky peaks

Hôtel Weisshorn to Gruben (via Cabane Bella-Tola)

V10B

Cabane Bella-Tola is a peaceful place to stay with excellent views

This is one of our favourite parts of the WHR. Although the paths leading to Cabane Bella-Tola are popular with day walkers, the scenery is sublime: wide open views of the valley below and the high peaks to the S including the Weisshorn (4506m), the Zinalrothorn (4221m), Dent Blanche (4357m) and the Matterhorn (4478m). The vista from Cabane Bella-Tola is particularly good and this makes for a wonderful overnight stop: much more relaxed and informal than Hôtel Weisshorn.

If you can believe it, the scenery gets even better after the cabane. After climbing through ski fields for about an hour, leave civilization behind and enter some of the most remote and beautiful terrain on the WHR. If the first part of the stage was busy, this section is anything but: most WHR walkers opt to use the standard route to Gruben described in Stage 10. Indeed, this is mountain walking at its finest. After passing the wonderful Lac de l'Armina (spectacularly set in a beautiful grassy bowl surrounded by peaks), climb to the awesome Meidpass where you enter German speaking territory. Here you will see that the best has been saved for last: descend through a wilderness of tarns and grassy slopes overlooked by snowy summits. Pass Meidsee, a magnificent lake, and then descend into the lovely Turtmanntal Valley. We cannot recommend this walk more highly.

The route to the cabane uses clear tracks and paths but route finding is a little fiddly. After Lac de la Bella-Tola, the terrain is remote so navigate carefully: this section should be avoided in low visibility or bad weather, when it would be easy to lose your way. The stage is well marked with red/white waymarks.

V10B

Meidpass Shortcut

From waypoint 1, TR and climb on a track. After 15min (2295m), TR onto a path. After 15min, TL at a fork: alternatively, TR for a short side trip to Lac de Combavert. Keep heading NE and 45min later, arrive at waypoint 9.

Total time: 1:15 between waypoints 1 and 9

The pretty hamlet of Mittelstafel

Meidsee is a beautiful little lake passed on the descent from the Meidpass

S See Map 10. From the hotel, head initially NE on a path ('Gruben'). After a few minutes, TL at a fork ('Gruben'). After 20min, cross a bridge and TL at a junction ('Gruben').

1 0:25: 5min later, arrive at the buildings of **le Chiesso**: to use the Meidpass Shortcut (see box), TR and climb. Otherwise, TL ('Chalet Blanc') and walk on a track. A few minutes later, TR at a fork ('Chalet Blanc').

2 0:35: TR on a path (no waymark). TR at the first fork.

3 0:45: From a junction just above **Chalet Blanc**, head N on a faint path ('Cabane Bella-Tola'). After a few minutes, TL down a track. Just afterwards, TR onto another track heading N: ignore offshoots.

4 1:15: At a bench, follow the track around to the right: do not take the path beginning in front of the bench. Shortly afterwards, TL on a path heading uphill (NW). Shortly, keep SH across a faint track and climb on a path ('Cabane Bella-Tola').

5 1:25: Arrive at **Cabane Bella-Tola (2346m)**. Behind the cabane, pick-up a path heading initially NE ('Lac de la Bella-Tola'). After 10min, keep SH across a track. After 10min, keep SH on a track. A few minutes later, TL on a path again. 10min later, pass some little lakes.

6 2:05: TL onto the track again ('Lac de la Bella-Tola'). After 10min, TR at a fork. Shortly afterwards, TR at a junction ('Lac de l'Armina'). Soon, pass the little **Lac de la Bella-Tola (2579m)**.

7 2:20: Just after a building, TL and climb on a path (easy to miss).

8 2:45: Follow the path around the left side of the magnificent **Lac de l'Armina (2562m)**. Afterwards, continue upwards on the path. When the path disappears, follow waymarks. There are a few sections of boulders to cross.

9 3:05: Keep SH at a junction ('Gruben'): this is where the Meidpass Shortcut rejoins Stage v10b.

10 3:30: Cross the **Meidpass (2789m)** and enter a new world: the views are exquisite. Descend on a clear path. After 20min, pass **Meidsee (2661m)**, a beautiful lake.

11 4:40: Descend on a track through the hamlet of **Oberstafel (2334m)**. Just afterwards, at a signpost, keep SH on a path ('Gruben'). 5min later, cross a track and descend on a path ('Gruben'). Shortly afterwards, follow the path through the lovely hamlet of **Mittelstafel (2267m)**, following waymarks.

12 5:25: TL on a track ('Gruben'). Shortly, cross a bridge. Immediately afterwards, TL and enter **Gruben (1818m)**.

11

On this exceptional stage, climb out of the Turtmanntal and over the Augstbordpass, the final col on the WHR. Then descend into the Mattertal Valley which will lead you triumphantly into Zermatt in a few days' time. The scenery throughout is fabulous with the highlight being one of the most beautiful viewpoints on the WHR (waypoint 6). From there, you can see the Mattertal Valley, the Ried Glacier and a variety of peaks, including the Dom (4545m) and the Täschhorn (4491m). It is a great place for a picnic. Afterwards, descend steeply to Jungen, a breathtaking little hamlet high above the Mattertal. Finally, drop into the valley at the town of St-Niklaus.

Take care on boulders before the Augstbordpass. And the final approach to the col is steep and unstable so watch your footing. Also, take care traversing boulders after waypoint no. 4.

Navigation on this stage would be tricky in low visibility or bad weather. When the path disappears over boulders, follow waymarks carefully to avoid losing the way.

The cable car from Jungen can be used to avoid the last part of the descent to St-Niklaus. See www.graechen.ch for opening times.

Accomodation at St-Niklaus is in short supply so book ahead. If you cannot get a bed then continue on to Grächen (Stage v12a) or Herbriggen (Stage v12c). Before leaving St-Niklaus, it is wise to check if the Europaweg is open (www.europaweg.ch).

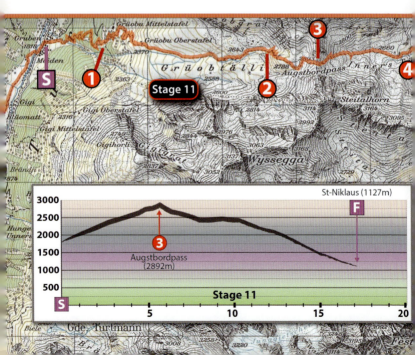

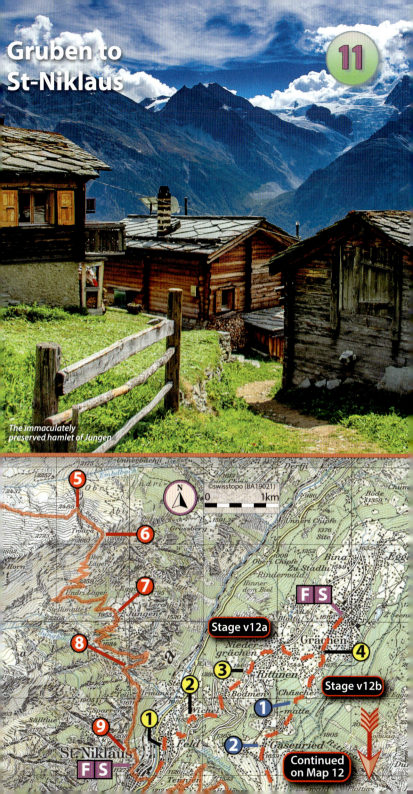

The immaculately preserved hamlet of Jungen

The magnificent viewpoint at waypoint no. 6

S From the hotel, head E, steeply uphill on a path ('St-Niklaus'). After 10min, keep SH at a junction.

1 0:35: Keep SH at a junction ('Augstbordpass'). After 15min, TL at a junction ('St-Niklaus'). 10min later, pass some farm buildings. After 10min, keep SH at a junction, heading E.

2 1:45: Climb steeply up a rocky slope. At times, cross boulders (waymarks). When the gradient eases again, you can see the col straight ahead. Descend briefly and then climb, across boulders, traversing the hillside (waymarks): it is easy to lose the route. After a few minutes, pick up a path again.

3 2:10: Cross the **Augstbordpass (2892m)** and descend on a path.

4 3:05: TR at a fork ('St-Niklaus'). Soon, the path crosses to the S side of the valley and then traverses E up its rocky flank: cross large sections of boulders (waymarks and cairns).

5 3:45: The path rounds a corner and contours SE around the slopes below the peak of Troära (2660m).

6 4:00: Arrive at one of the most beautiful viewpoints on the WHR. 5min later, TL at a junction ('Jungen'). After 15min, TL at another junction. A few minutes later, TR at a junction ('St-Niklaus'). After 10-15min, keep SH at a junction (no sign). When you can see Jungen just below, keep on the main path through trees, ignoring offshoots.

7 4:55: Arrive at the hamlet of **Jungen (1955m)**. Follow a path down through the incredible old buildings following signs for 'St-Niklaus'. TR at the chapel and continue descending. Now simply follow the signs for 'St-Niklaus'.

8 5:45: Keep SH at a junction ('St Niklaus'). Shortly afterwards, cross a bridge. A few minutes later, TL at a fork, continuing downhill ('St-Niklaus').

9 6:10: TL at a junction ('Bahnhof'). Descend to a cable car station and then follow a road down to the train station in **St-Niklaus (1127m)**. TL through a tunnel, under the tracks, to head into the town.

Time	7:15
Distance	17.1
Ascent	1096
Descent	1787
Maximum Altitude	2892
Refreshments on route	St-Niklaus
Accommodation	St-Niklaus

Walkers climb out of the Turtmanntal Valley towards the Augstbordpass

Time	7:45
Distance	17.2
Ascent	1862
Descent	725
Maximum Altitude	2696
Refreshments on route	Europahütte
Accommodation	Europahütte

The incomparable Europaweg

St-Niklaus to the Europahütte

12

The Europaweg crosses some unstable terrain

The Europaweg, travelled on Stages 12, 13a and 13b, is a clear highlight of the WHR. It is a high altitude balcony path heading S down the Mattertal Valley in the shadow of a large array of famous Swiss peaks. To the E, the 4,000m summits include the Dom (4545m) and the Täschhorn (4491m). However, the views of the Weisshorn (4506m) and the Zinalrothorn (4221m) on the W side of the valley are just incredible. And then there are the glaciers. Oh the glaciers! They are everywhere!

That was the good news. The bad news is that the Europaweg is very tough: the permanently undulating path is often rocky and uneven and sometimes non-existent. It is much tougher than it looks on paper. Furthermore, before setting out on Stage 12, you should be fully aware of the risks involved: see below. If in doubt, proceed to Zermatt by way of Stages v12c and v13.

The Europaweg's lofty position, cut into the face of the cliffs, means that it is prone to landslides and rockfalls. Accordingly, the path is frequently closed and the exact route changes regularly as repairs are made or destroyed sections are re-routed. As a result, the path on the ground may differ from the directions given below. Use of the Europaweg carries risk: huge sections of it are narrow, rocky and unstable and the drops are sheer. Falling rocks could cause injury or death. If you do decide to walk it, then move as quickly as safety allows through exposed sections. And only stop for a break in places where you are not at risk from falling rocks. It would be unwise to attempt it in bad weather, poor visibility or after rain (when landslides and rockfalls are more likely). Some of the most exposed sections are protected with fixed chains or ropes. If at any time you find that the route is blocked, then turn back.

For the entire stage, follow signs for Zermatt. Do not set out on the Europaweg unless you have a booking for the Europahütte: the subsequent accommodation is at Randa (all the way down on the valley floor) or at Täschalp (4hr away on Stage 13a). The regular bus service from St-Niklaus to Gasenried could be used to avoid the first part of the climb: pick the route up at waypoint 2 of Stage v12b. See www.graechen.ch for bus timetables. Before leaving St-Niklaus, it is wise to check if the Europaweg is open (www.europaweg.ch).

The stunning viewpoint near Grat

S See Map 12. From the train station, walk down a cobbled street past the post office. TR onto 'Dorfstrasse'. Then take the first left, heading downhill on a narrow street. Cross a road onto 'Eyeweg'. Soon, cross a bridge over the river. Immediately afterwards, TR on a path and climb. Shortly, TL at two forks. Then TR onto a track

1 0:20: After two hairpins, turn sharp left onto a path heading NE. TR at the next two junctions. A few minutes later, TL onto a track.

2 1:10: A few minutes after the third hairpin, TL on a path and head through the hamlet of **Hellenen (1523m)**. Soon, ignore a path descending to the left and climb into forest. 5min later, TL at a junction.

3 1:30: TR before a bridge onto the Europaweg. Soon, climb steeply: keep on the main path ignoring offshoots.

4 2:15: TR at a junction.

5 2:55: Arrive at a lovely plateau. Shortly afterwards, climb a short section of rocks. Then TL at a junction ('Zermatt'). 5min from the plateau, arrive at the wonderful viewpoint at **Grat (2335m)**, one of the finest on the WHR. TL and keep climbing (waymarks and cairns).

6 3:30: Pass the **statue of St Bernard (2474m)** which commemorates the opening of the Europaweg in 1997.

7 4:00: Keep SH at a junction. Soon afterwards, the terrain becomes more challenging with precipitous scree slopes. Take great care crossing **Grosse Grabe**, a huge ravine of unstable boulders: move as fast as safety permits because there is a risk of rockfall here. After crossing the boulders, use a rope and steps to climb some steep rocks. Descend briefly and then cross another boulder field: there are sections of wooden walkways to assist.

8 6:00: At a junction at **Galenburg (2580m)**, keep on the higher path: do not descend. After contouring around the slopes of a valley, descend to around 2300m. Then contour around the slopes again. There are a number of streams to cross on bridges: take care as these are often destroyed or damaged by rockfall. If in doubt, do not cross.

F 7:45: Arrive at the **Europahütte (2264m)**.

Be sure to book the amazing Europahütte in advance

12

A bird's eye view of St-Niklaus from near Grächen

S See Map 11. From the train station, walk down a cobbled street past the post office. TR onto 'Dorfstrasse'. Then take the first left, heading downhill on a narrow street. Cross a road onto 'Eyeweg'. Soon, cross a bridge over the river. Immediately afterwards, TL on a small road.

(1) 0:15: Cross a main road and keep SH on a small road ('Grächen'). 5min later, TR. Immediately afterwards TL and continue on another small road ('Grächen').

(2) 0:30: At the hamlet of **Wichel (1185m)**, bear right onto a small road. Shortly afterwards, TL at a junction. After 5min, cross a road and continue uphill on a narrow path on the other side: ignore the confusing signpost. Cross the road again and continue uphill on a path. At the hamlet of **Bodmen (1358m)**, cross a road and continue on a tarmac lane. Shortly afterwards, TL ('Grächen').

(3) 1:05: Keep SH on a road. Shortly afterwards, TL on a tarmac lane (yellow sign). After a few minutes, keep SH to climb on a path (yellow signs). TL onto the road again. Shortly afterwards, TR on a path just before the little chapel at **Niedergrächen (1478m)**.

(4) 1:40: TL onto a street.

F 1:45: Arrive in **Grächen (1619m)**.

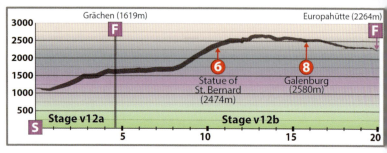

St-Niklaus to Grächen

V12A

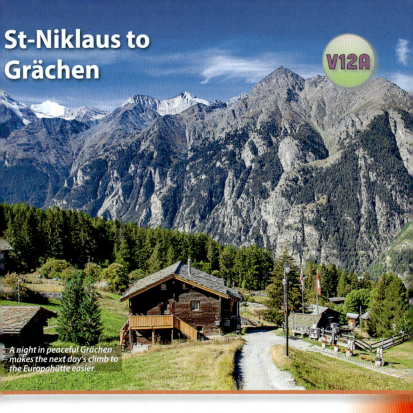

A night in peaceful Grächen makes the next day's climb to the Europahütte easier

A very pleasant climb to the relaxing village of Grächen. Accomodation at St-Niklaus is in short supply but there are plenty of options in Grächen. This stage could be tagged onto Stage 11 although it does make for a long day. Alternatively, there is a regular bus from St-Niklaus to Grächen (see www.graechen.ch). Spending the night in Grächen has the added advantage of substantially reducing the climb on the next day's tough stage to the Europahütte.

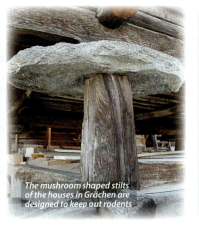

The mushroom shaped stilts of the houses in Grächen are designed to keep out rodents

Time	1:45
Distance	4.6
Ascent	540
Descent	48
Maximum Altitude	1619
Refreshments on route	Grächen
Accommodation	Grächen

The little hamlet of Gasenried is near the start of the Europaweg

Grächen to the Europahütte

V12B

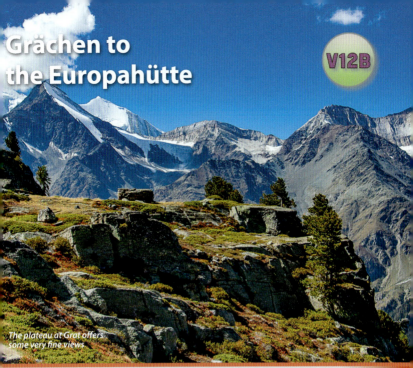

The plateau at Grat offers some very fine views

This variant route to the Europahütte is for those who stay overnight in Grächen. The information in the introduction to Stage 12 applies equally to Stage v12b. In particular, read the warnings there concerning the Europaweg before setting out.

S See Map 11. From the chapel, walk SW down the main street of Grächen. 5min later, TL at a fork ('Gasenried').

1 0:20: TR at a junction (unsigned) and cross a ravine. 5min later, near some buildings, TL at a fork ('Gasenried') onto a path. A few minutes later, TL onto a road.

2 0:30: See Map 12. Enter **Gasenried (1659m)**, passing a little supermarket and a hotel (closed). From the chapel, head S on a road. Pass a restaurant. Just afterwards, TR at a fork, continuing on the road.

3 0:40: TL onto the Europweg at waypoint 3 of Stage 12. Follow the Stage 12 directions to the Europahütte.

F 6:55: Arrive at the **Europahütte (2264m)**.

Gasenried used to have a hotel but it is permanently closed. Before departing, it is wise to check if the Europaweg is open (www.europaweg.ch).

Time	7:00
Distance	15.5
Ascent	1376
Descent	731
Maximum Altitude	2696
Refreshments on route	Gasenried (0:35) Europahütte
Accommodation	Europahütte

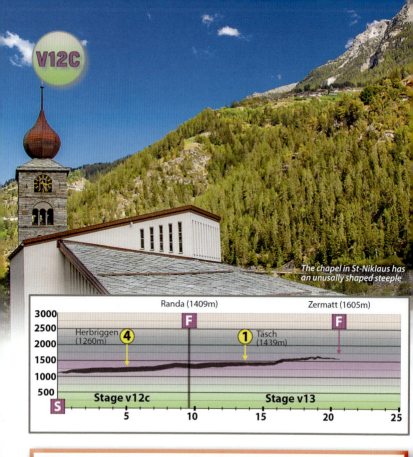

The chapel in St-Niklaus has an unusally shaped steeple

S See Map 12. From the train station, walk down a cobbled street past the post office. TR onto Dorfstrasse. On arrival at the main road, TR ('Herbriggen').

1 0:10: TR up a road ('Herbriggen'). Soon, pass under the railway tracks.

2 0:25: Head through the hamlet of **Ze Schwidernu (1163m)**. Soon pass under the railway again. Immediately afterwards, TR on a small road running parallel to the tracks.

3 0:50: Arrive at the main road at **Mattsand (1227m)**. Before the chapel, cross the railway and continue on a small road ('Herbriggen'). Shortly afterwards, TR at a fork (yellow waymarks). After a reservoir, bear right on a track.

4 1:20: Arrive at a junction: if you wish to continue directly to Randa, keep SH and soon reach waypoint no. 5. To head into **Herbriggen (1260m)**, TL, pass through a tunnel and then climb to the main street. From the hotel in Herbriggen, head S down the road. Soon, cross the main road and descend to the train station. Take care crossing the tracks and descend to the river. Cross a bridge.

5 1:30: Immediately afterwards, TL on a track ('Randa'). After 15min, TL at the hamlet of **Zenackern (1261m)** and cross a bridge over the river. Immediately afterwards, TR on a track alongside the railway. Keep SH when the track becomes a tarmac lane.

6 2:25: TR at a fork onto a road. Just after passing under the main road, TR.

F 2:30: Arrive at the station in **Randa (1409m)**.

St-Niklaus to Randa (via Herbriggen)

V12C

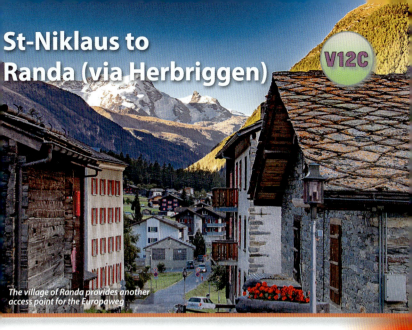

The village of Randa provides another access point for the Europaweg

This valley walk is useful if the Stage 12 section of the Europaweg is closed, the weather is bad or you are short of time. The walk is pleasant but an anti-climax after the trekking enjoyed over the previous days. Nevertheless, after Mattsand, there are superb views of the Breithorn (4164m). Take care crossing the railway lines at Mattsand and Herbriggen. The hotel at Herbriggen has some excellent dormitories which have been recently refurbished.

If short of time, consider taking the train from St-Niklaus to Randa (see www.sbb.ch for timetables). From Randa, there are four options:

1. Head directly to Zermatt along the valley floor (Stage v13): useful if the Stage 13a section of the Europaweg is closed or in bad weather;
2. Climb to the Europahütte and spend the night there (Stage v12d);
3. Climb to the Charles Kuonen Suspension Bridge (Stage v12d) and then walk Stage 13a; and
4. Get the train from Randa to Zermatt.

Time	2:30
Distance	9.6
Ascent	329
Descent	47
Maximum Altitude	1409
Refreshments on route	Herbriggen (1:25) Randa
Accommodation	Herbriggen (1:25) Randa

The Charles Kuonen Bridge is the longest pedestrian suspension bridge in the world

Time	2:30
Distance	4.0
Ascent	866
Descent	11
Maximum Altitude	2264
Refreshments on route	Europahütte
Accommodation	Europahütte

Randa to the Europahütte

V12D

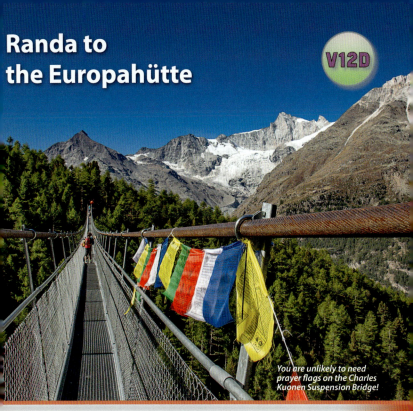

You are unlikely to need prayer flags on the Charles Kuonen Suspension Bridge!

Even if the Stage 12 part of the Europaweg is closed, you may still be able to walk the Stage 13 sections: use Stage v12d to climb to the Charles Kuonen Suspension Bridge and then pass onto Stage 13a. Alternatively, you could use Stage v12d to climb to the Europahütte, overnight there and then walk Stages 13a and 13b the following day. The climb is steep in places.

S See Map 12. From the train station and tourist office, head SE along a road. After a few minutes, TL up another road ('Europahütte'). TL after the chapel. Immediately afterwards, TR ('Europahütte') and climb on a cobbled street past some incredible traditional buildings. 15min from the start, TL at a junction ('Europahütte'). Soon you will glimpse the famous suspension bridge up to the right.

1 0:30: After 5min, TL onto a tarmac lane and cross a bridge. Afterwards, bear right and pick up a path ('Europahütte'), initially heading NE. Head either left or right at the first fork. 5min later, TR ('Europahütte') and climb steeply.

2 1:15: TL at a junction. Just afterwards, keep SH at another junction ('Europahütte').

3 1:55: Arrive at a junction beside the **Charles Kuonen Suspension Bridge**: keep SH for the Europahütte (or TL to cross the bridge and continue on Stage 13a). After 25min, TL at a junction ('Europahütte').

F 2:30: Arrive at the **Europahütte (2264m)**.

139

On Stage 13a the Matterhorn finally shows its famous crooked form

The Europahütte to Täschalp

13A

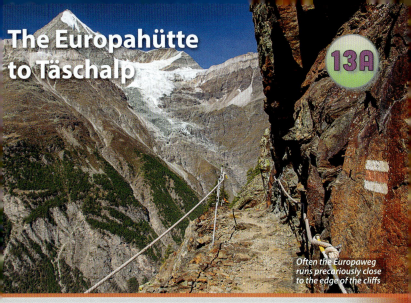

Often the Europaweg runs precariously close to the edge of the cliffs

Unbelievably, Stages 13a and 13b are scenically superior to Stage 12. There are more great views of the Weisshorn (4506m) and the Zinalrothorn (4221m) on the W side of the valley. However, the Matterhorn (4478m) will soon command much of your attention: as you get closer to Zermatt, it changes shape before your eyes from a wedge to the iconic crooked form immortalized in a billion photos. Pray for good weather as these are the scenes that you have been dreaming about since Chamonix. Stages 13a and 13b are probably the overall highlight of, and a fitting climax to, the WHR.

The information in the introduction to Stage 12 applies equally to Stage 13a. In particular, read the warnings there concerning the Europaweg before setting out. There are many narrow and precipitous sections with steep drops throughout the day: take great care as a fall would be serious. On narrow sections, particularly those with overhanging rocks, do not rest as it is possible that rocks could fall from above. There is also a long section of concrete overhangs: at the time of writing, some sections of the overhang had collapsed. Move as quickly as safety permits and keep well underneath the overhangs to ensure that any falling rocks do not hit you. Follow signs for 'Zermatt' throughout the stage.

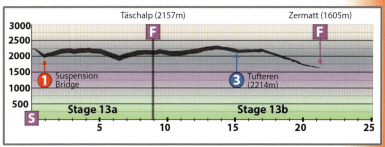

141

The Europaweg near Täschalp

The Charles Kuonen Suspension Bridge (Hängebrücke)

It is the longest pedestrian suspension bridge in the world and takes about 10min to cross. Situated above Randa at an altitude of 2070m, it is 494m long and 85m above the valley at its highest point. It was constructed using 8 tonnes of cables and has a special system that prevents swinging. The bridge is part of the famous hiking path, the Europaweg, between Grächen and Zermatt. It was built to replace the previous bridge, the shorter Europabrücke. The metal grating you walk upon allows you to see right down to the valley floor: it is exhilarating but is perhaps best avoided if you have a fear of heights. If you do not wish to cross, you can descend to Randa, following Stage v12d in reverse.

Time	3:30
Distance	8.9
Ascent	512
Descent	619
Maximum Altitude	2264
Refreshments on route	Täschalp
Accommodation	Täschalp

Savouring the Europaweg

S Take the path heading S and descend, initially over boulders. After 5min, TR at a junction.

1 0:20: Cross the **Charles Kuonen Suspension Bridge** (see box). After the bridge, keep SH on a path. After a few minutes, TL at a junction and climb. A few minutes later, TR at another junction. The Weisshorn (4506m) is the huge peak to your right. Keep SH at another junction. Just afterwards, views become more expansive and you should see the Matterhorn just starting to poke out to the SW. Soon, cross some boulders. Then take care on a narrow section protected with ropes.

2 1:10: TR at a fork. Immediately afterwards, TL at another fork. Shortly afterwards, descend steeply through a roped section. Then the path makes its way precipitously around the edge of the cliffs: take care. Pass through a tunnel: it is dark but there are light switches on timers.

3 1:55: Pass a grassy area which is the first good place to stop since the Europahütte. Shortly afterwards, keep SH at a junction and cross some boulders. Soon, start to descend.

4 2:20: Walk underneath a section of concrete overhangs (see above). Just after the overhangs, start to climb again. A few minutes later, TL at a fork.

F 3:30: TL on a road, cross a bridge and enter the hamlet of **Täschalp (2157m).** Keep SH to the lovely **Europaweg-Hütte** (not to be confused with the 'Europahütte').

143

13B

The amazing views resume immediately after leaving Täschalp

S See Map 13a. TR on a path beside the Europaweg-Hütte. Soon, cross the river and climb on the other side.

1 0:30: Keep SH at a junction. 10min later, climb through a cabled section. Soon, TL at a fork, continuing to climb on a track, enjoying incredible views.

2 1:20: Head around a corner where there is a magnificent view of the Matterhorn. Then start to descend gently. After 20min, keep SH at a signpost. After a few minutes, TR at a fork (no waymarks).

3 1:55: A few minutes later, arrive at the hamlet of **Tufteren (2214m)** where there is a restaurant. If short of time, you can descend directly to Zermatt from here. However, to continue on the Europaweg, TL and follow signs for 'Sunnegga'. After 15min, TL at a fork.

4 2:20: TL at the ski station of **Sunnegga (2288m)** and descend on a track ('Zermatt'). Shortly afterwards, follow the track around to the right. Just afterwards, TL onto a path ('Findeln-eggen')

5 2:40: TR and head through the hamlet of **Findeln-eggen**. Now follow signs for 'Winkelmatten'. After 10min, in the hamlet of **Ze Gassu**, keep SH at a junction: do not TL even though it is also signed to 'Winkelmatten'. At the next fork, TL ('Winkelmatten').

6 3:20: Cross the Gornergrat railway track and continue down a path. TR onto a lane and arrive at **Winkelmatten (1672m)**. TR by the chapel and descend on a small road: there are some footpaths you can use to cut corners.

F 3:40: Arrive at the river at the bottom of **Zermatt**. Well done: you have completed the WHR. Cross the bridge and climb to head for the centre of town.

Täschalp to Zermatt

13B

The Matterhorn provides an incredible climax to an exceptional trek

The non-stop views of the Matterhorn provide a wonderful climax to the WHR. This is what you came to see and the quality of the views is in no way exaggerated. It is worth noting that those who spend the night at Täschalp, and start Stage 13b early, often get the best photographs: by afternoon, the sun will be directly above the Matterhorn which can cause glare. After a long and magnificent balcony path, make the long descent into Zermatt to complete the WHR.

Unless otherwise indicated, follow signs for 'Zermatt' throughout. The descent from Sunnegga to Zermatt is another knee-jerker. You can avoid it by taking the funicular railway from Sunnegga right into the heart of Zermatt. For timetables see www.matterhornparadise.ch.

Tufteren

Time	3:45
Distance	12.3
Ascent	298
Descent	850
Maximum Altitude	2347
Refreshments on route	Tufteren (1:55) Sunnegga (2:20) Ze Gassu (2:50) Zermatt
Accommodation	Zermatt

145

The old Valaisian buildings of Zermatt: the Matterhorn is emerging from the cloud behind

Randa to Zermatt (via Täsch)

V13

Walkers on the valley trail just outside Zermatt

S See Map 13a. From the train station, head NW on a road. Soon, bear left and pass under the road. Shortly afterwards, TL to cross the train tracks and a bridge over the River Matter Vispa. Immediately afterwards, TL on a path alongside the river. 20min from the start, cross a bridge over the river. Immediately afterwards, cross back again. Soon, the riverside path passes a golf course.

① 1:20: Keep SH past the campsite at **Täsch (1439m)**: alternatively, TL and cross the bridge if you need supplies. After 30min, TL onto another path and climb. 5min later, TR at a fork.

② 1:50: TR at a fork and climb. Soon Zermatt comes into view ahead.

③ 2:25: Keep SH past a heliport which is a constant hive of activity. 5min later, keep SH at a junction for the centre of Zermatt: alternatively, you can TL to go directly to the train station. Keep SH on a road overlooking the rooftops of the town. When the road ends, TL down an alley.

F 2:45: Arrive at the main street of **Zermatt (1605m)**.

Another valley walk which is useful if the Stage 13a/13b section of the Europaweg is closed, the weather is bad or you are short of time. This stage is more enjoyable than Stage v12c (St-Niklaus to Randa). If short of time, consider taking the train from Randa to Zermatt (see www.sbb.ch for timetables). Follow signs for Zermatt throughout.

Time	2:45
Distance	11.1
Ascent	281
Descent	85
Maximum Altitude	1645
Refreshments on route	Täsch (1:20) Zermatt
Accommodation	Täsch (1:20) Zermatt

Gornergrat to Riffelalp (Walk no. 23)

This is a Zermatt 'must see' with some exceptional views of the Matterhorn and a host of glaciers. The ride to the start on the historic Gornergrat railway is a treat in itself: best views on the right side of the train. This walk is simply unforgettable and you can enjoy it at your leisure as the route is almost entirely downhill.

Time: 3:00

Distance: 9.5km

Ascent/Descent: 150m/1020m

Refreshments: Gornergrat, Riffelberg, Riffelalp

Start: Gornergrat (Gornergrat railway from Zermatt). **Finish:** Riffelalp (take Gornergrat railway back to Zermatt)

Edelweissweg (Walk no. 30)

On a fine day, this route will be a highlight of your walking career: it is the equal of any hike in the Alps. A long climb to Trift leads to the awesomely long Höhbalmen balcony path, a stone's throw from the Matterhorn. Afterwards, descend to Zermatt via the lovely hamlet of Zmutt. Because the climb cannot be avoided using transport, the route is less trodden and is normally peaceful.

Time: 7:30

Distance: 20.6km

Ascent/Descent: 1140m/1140m

Refreshments: Edelweiss Alterhaupt, Trift, Zmutt

Start/Finish: Zermatt (no transport)

The Five Lakes (Walk no. 11)

An easy but magnificent walk around the tarns near Sunnegga. It passes many of the classic Matterhorn viewpoints with stunning reflections of the mountain in the lakes. The route can also be accessed directly from Stage 13b of the WHR: signposts to the lakes from Sunnegga.

Time: 2:30

Distance: 8km

Ascent/Descent: 160m/450m

Refreshments: Blauherd, Ze Seewjinen, Sunnegga

Start: Blauherd (funicular railway and cable car from Zermatt). **Finish:** Sunnegga (funicular railway back to Zermatt)

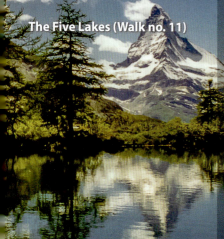

Zermatt Day Walks

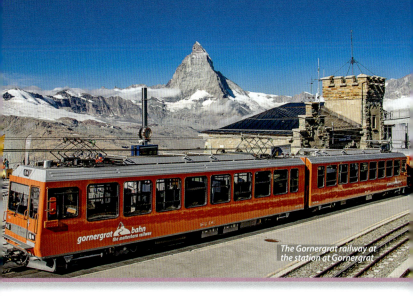
The Gornergrat railway at the station at Gornergrat

There are plenty of mountain towns in the Alps but there are none quite like Zermatt. Set in a bowl near the top of the Mattertal Valley, it is surrounded by magnificent 4000m peaks including the queen of them all, the iconic Matterhorn (4478m). The unusual crooked shape of the Matterhorn and its position, standing regally apart from its peers, draw the eye as you walk around the town. The mountain is absolutely integral to the character and atmosphere of Zermatt: it is easy to see why many people leave the town completely unaware of the names of any of the other high summits such as the Breithorn (4164m), Monte Rosa (4553m), the Dent Blanche (4357m) or the Zinalrothorn (4221m), to name a few. And in fact, the Matterhorn is so famous that it has three names: Matterhorn (German), Monte Cervino (Italian) and Mont Cervin (French).

But the Matterhorn alone is not what makes a stay in Zermatt so special: just as important is the unparalleled network of trains and cable cars that whisk the visitor into the heart of the mountains. They are expensive but they make the most incredible walking available to all without too much effort: exactly what you need after the rigours of the WHR.

The network of walking paths is exceptional and the routes are all numbered and displayed on the free map available at the tourist office in Zermatt. A day or two on these paths will be an incredible finale to an incredible trek. In fact, you could easily spend a month exploring them but, to make life easy for you, we have featured three of the best in this section. The walk numbers are those used on the tourist office map.

Mont Blanc basking in the morning sun

Notes

Your Next Trek?

THE GREAT TREKS OF THE ALPS

The Tour of the Écrins National Park

The GR54 is a stunning walk in the French Alps, taking 9 to 12 days, through some of the wildest mountain terrain in the world

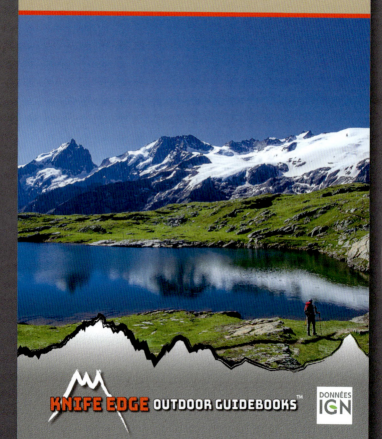

KNIFE EDGE OUTDOOR GUIDEBOOKS

DONNÉES IGN

We thought guidebooks were boring so we decided to change them. Mapping is better than 40 years ago. Graphics are better than 40 years ago. Photography is better than 40 years ago. So why have walking guidebooks remained the same?

Well our guidebooks are **different**:

- **We use Real Maps.** You know, the **1:25,000/1:50,000** scale maps that walkers actually use to navigate with. Not sketch maps that get you lost. Real maps make more work for us but we think it is worth it. You don't need to buy separate maps so we save you money! And you are less likely to get lost so we save you time!

- **Numbered Waypoints** on our Real Maps link to the walk descriptions, making routes easier to follow than traditional text based guides. No more wading through pages of boring words to find out where you are! You want to look at mountains and not have your face stuck in a book all day. Right?

- **Colour, colour, colour.** Mountains are **beautiful** so guidebooks should be too. We were fed up using guidebooks which were ugly and boring. When we are planning, we want to be **dazzled** with full size colour pictures of the **magnificence** which awaits us! So our guidebooks fill every inch of the page with beauty: big, **spectacular** photos of mountains. Oh yeah baby!

- **More practical size.** Long and slim. Long enough to have Real Maps and large pictures but slim enough to fit in a pocket.

Now all that sounds great to us but we want to know if you like what we have done. So hit us with your feedback: good or bad. We are not too proud to change.

Follow us for trek updates, discount coupons and other interesting trekking stuff.

 www.knifeedgeoutdoor.com

 info@knifeedgeoutdoor.com

 @knifeedgeoutdoor

 @knifeedgeout

 @knifeedgeoutdoor

Could you write a guidebook?

Knife Edge is always on the lookout for talent. If you think you could author a Knife Edge walking or mountain biking guidebook, then email us a summary of your project and some sample photos. We will review them to see if they are of interest. Any decision is in our absolute discretion. Good luck!

Swiss Map Mobile

Wherever it suits you, online as well as offline, safely under way

Schweizerische Eidgenossenschaft
Confédération suisse
Confederazione Svizzera
Confederaziun svizra

Swiss Confederation

Federal Office of Topography swisstopo
www.swisstopo.ch

www.swisstopo.ch/smm